Praise for *Artisan Bread in Five Minutes a Day* and *The New Artisan Bread in Five Minutes a Day*

"Soon the bread will be baking itself . . . The crusty, full-flavored loaf that results may be the world's easiest yeast bread."
—*The New York Times*

"If man cannot live by bread alone, it may be because Jeff Hertzberg and Zoë François didn't publish their book sooner. . . . [They've] developed a method that makes any home into a mini artisan bake shop . . . Hertzberg and François's practical, common-sense method . . . is, quite simply, genius."
—*Chicago Tribune*

"Every step of Zoë and Jeff's adventures in bread has been fascinating and delicious for us, the home bread bakers who follow them, but this book might be their most exciting yet because they've incorporated years of readers' questions, problems, and discoveries into every chapter. This is truly the all-you've-ever-wanted-to-know edition. And there are plenty of photographs at last!"
—**Dorie Greenspan, James Beard Award–winning author of *Around My French Table***

"If holiday gift-givers are aiming to buy one new cookbook title for the bakers in their lives, they should look no further."
—*Minneapolis Star Tribune*

"Is it possible for an inexperienced baker to make some of the best bread imaginable in just five minutes of active time in the kitchen? We didn't think it was possible . . . all our preconceived notions of what it takes to make fantastic bread became instantly out-dated."
—*Portland Oregonian*

"So let me cut to the chase: I may have found the holy grail of bread making, folks . . . Hertzberg and François's method is a home run, making the intimidating and mythical a done (and tasty) deal."
—*The Washington Post*

"Of the 20 best recipes in the history of *The Splendid Table* . . . Number 1: Five Minute Artisan Bread, Jeff Hertzberg and Zoë François."
—*The Splendid Table*

Praise for *Healthy Bread in Five Minutes a Day*

"Zoë François and Jeff Hertzberg have amazingly demystified the arcane and delightful world of artisan bread. Now, on the heels of time sensitivity (Hello . . . 5 minutes??? Really? Yes!), comes a baking book for the health-conscious, and it couldn't be more timely. Bottom line, I would crawl across a desert of broken glass to hop into their loaf pan."

—Andrew Zimmern

"It's a vast improvement over the laborious process of making artisan breads using classic methods . . . [In] their new book, Hertzberg and François have gone one step further . . . baking breads that use less sugar, healthy grains, fruits and vegetables, and are friendly to those with allergies or food sensitivities."

—Associated Press

"We tried some of the recipes; we love 'em. . . . Honestly, this is the nicest, softest whole wheat sandwich bread I've ever made."

—KingArthurBaking.com

"This is the much-anticipated sequel to the wildly popular *Artisan Bread in Five Minutes a Day* . . . you'll be able to use the no-knead storage dough method with even healthier recipes . . . fabulous cookbooks . . . yummy but easy recipes!"

—*Mother Earth News*

"*Healthy Bread in Five Minutes a Day* . . . is a cookbook that just might change your life . . . Brilliant? I say yes! I sometimes read cookbooks like novels, and this book . . . is filled with good ideas about healthy bread baking."

—*Glamour.com*

Praise for *Gluten-Free Artisan Bread in Five Minutes a Day*

"Quick artisan breads, no kneading, no proofing, no punching down . . . You'll be on your way to delicious bread in no time."

—*Living Free's Gluten Free & More Magazine*

"For gluten-free bread that tastes like it came from a European bakery, it's worth the wait."

—*The Oregonian*

"I baked a flatbread for a gluten-free friend—and no one suspected it was not its floury cousin . . . The book's recipes for blending your own gluten-free flours are easy and fail-safe." —*Minneapolis Star Tribune*

"Hertzberg and François offer foolproof recipes for [gluten-free] bread . . ." —*The Columbus Dispatch*

"The recipes make you wonder why you use wheat when such fabulous bread can be made without it . . . We can personally vouch for the doughnuts. OMG." —*Minneapolis–St. Paul City Pages*

Praise for *Artisan Pizza and Flatbread in Five Minutes a Day*

"A wealth of information on how to prepare this world-famous dish in minutes . . . an outstanding book for working parents that are interested in serving healthier meals to their families during the week." —*Seattle Post-Intelligencer*

"Will get the baker on your list jumping with glee. Thin crust, thick crust, dipping breads and desserts—think good old pizza margherita, Turkish pita boats, and banana cream hand pies—all in the time it takes to heat up the oven." —**Associated Press**

"You want this book . . . endless variations in pizza crusts, sauces, and toppings, plus troubleshooting tips and instructions on tossing pies pizza parlor–style right in your own kitchen." —*Mother Earth News*

"It sounds too good to be true, but [*Artisan Pizza and Flatbread in Five Minutes a Day*] . . . has a technique to prep the dough that will make you wonder why you've been buying pizza dough." —*McClatchy-Tribune*

"[Their first book] . . . banished the fear of kneading for a whole generation of cooks. Now, with their newest adventure the duo takes on an even bigger task: that completely personal and often polarizing topic—crust . . . with a truckload of recipes that are exciting and intriguing to even the casual pizza maker. Basically, it's a reason to broaden your pizza boundaries and become the pizzaioli you've always dreamed of being."
—*Mpls.St.Paul Magazine*

"It doesn't get any easier than this . . . thin-crust pizza? Jeff and Zoë to the rescue, again! No special skills needed, no fancy ingredients, no hard-to-find ingredients . . . Sicilian style? Awesome—chewy, crunchy crust, full of big holes, and perfectly cooked toppings."
—KingArthurBaking.com

The Best of
ARTISAN BREAD
in Five Minutes a Day

The Best of
ARTISAN BREAD
in Five Minutes a Day

Favorite Recipes from BreadIn5

JEFF HERTZBERG, M.D., **and** ZOË FRANÇOIS

Photography by STEPHEN SCOTT GROSS

ST. MARTIN'S PRESS ✺ NEW YORK

First published in the United States by St. Martin's Press, an imprint of St. Martin's Publishing Group

THE BEST OF ARTISAN BREAD IN FIVE MINUTES A DAY. Copyright © 2021 by Jeff Hertzberg and Zoë François. Photographs copyright © 2021 by Stephen Scott Gross.

Contains some material previously published in the BreadIn5 series.

www.stmartins.com

Library of Congress Cataloging-in-Publication Data

Names: Hertzberg, Jeff, author. | François, Zoë, author.
Title: The best of Artisan bread in five minutes a day : favorite recipes
   from BreadIn5 / Jeff Hertzberg, M.D. and Zoë François ; photography by
   Stephen Scott Gross.
Description: First edition. | New York : St. Martin's Press, 2021. |
   Includes index.
Identifiers: LCCN 2021026575 | ISBN 9781250277435 (hardcover) | ISBN
   9781250277442 (ebook)
Subjects: LCSH: Cooking (Bread) | Bread. | LCGFT: Cookbooks.
Classification: LCC TX769 .H4744 2021 | DDC 641.81/5--dc23
LC record available at https://lccn.loc.gov/2021026575

Our books may be purchased in bulk for promotional, educational, or business use. Please contact your local bookseller or the Macmillan Corporate and Premium Sales Department at 1-800-221-7945, extension 5442, or by email at MacmillanSpecialMarkets@macmillan.com.

First Edition: 2021

10 9 8 7 6 5 4 3 2 1

To our readers who told us the real secret: which breads they bake every day.

Jeff

To the BreadIn5 community of bakers who shared their love of baking with us over the years.

Zoë

CONTENTS

〜〜

Acknowledgments ix

The Secret xiii

Foreword by Andrew Zimmern xv

1 Introduction 1

2 Ingredients 11

3 Equipment 27

4 Tips and Techniques 41

5 The Master Recipe 63

6 More Basic Doughs 79

7 Classic Shapes with Master and Basic Doughs 85

8 Loaves from Around the World 117

9 Pizza and Flatbreads 157

10 Gluten-Free Breads 171

11 Enriched Breads and Pastries 187

12 Natural Sourdough Starter (Levain) 231

   Sources for Bread-Baking Products 243

   Index 245

ACKNOWLEDGMENTS

This has been a long and wonderful road, stretching back over fifteen years, and that gives us a lot of people to thank. First, thanks to Peter Wolverton, our editor at St. Martin's Press, for another great effort, and for supporting our seven previous titles. Lynne Rossetto Kasper took Jeff's call (a thinly veiled book pitch) on *The Splendid Table* radio show in 2000, and the late great Ruth Cavin, our very first editor, asked for a book proposal based on little more than faith and intuition.

Our wonderful literary agent, Jane Dystel, and her fantastic team—Miriam Goderich and Lauren Abramo—shepherded our books here in the United States, and introduced them to readers in Britain, Germany, China, Taiwan, and Japan. Jeff Lin of BustOutSolutions.com maintains our website, where we have the privilege of connecting directly with our readers.

Bill Hanes, Kelly Olson, and Linda Nelson of Red Star Yeast have been great believers in our method, ever since Bill and Kelly saw our demo at a Milwaukee book signing, and embarked on a long partnership, helping us get the word out about fast yeasted breads. Peggy Orenstein, Beth Fouhy, and Danny Sager have helped us navigate the magical world of literary public relations ever since our first book—we wouldn't be here without them. Hannah Smith, Ph.D., helped us understand the biology of yeast, Alexandra Cohn critiqued our rye breads, and Riv-Ellen Prell and Steven Foldes did the same for challahs. The great team at Craftsy (now MyBlueprint.com) produced Zoë's fabulous instructional video, "Artisan Bread in Minutes."

It really takes a village to raise a cookbook. Friends lent Herculean talents and support: Jen Sommerness; Craig and Patricia Neal; Lorraine Neal; Leslie Bazzett; Jay, Tracey, Gavin, and Megan Berkowitz; the late Sarah Berkowitz; the late Barbara Neal; Marion and John Callahan; Barb Davis; Fran Davis; Anna and Ewart François; Kathy Kasnoff and Lyonel Norris; Andy Small; Andrew Hachiya; Troy Meyers; Kristin Neal and Bill Friedman; Carey, Heather, and Victoria Neal; Sally Simmons and David van de Sande; and Amy Vang.

Gratitude to colleagues in our baking and culinary adventures past and present: Robin Asbell; Steven Brown of Tilia and St. Genevieve; Adam Cohn of Adam Cohn Law; Abby Dodge; Stephen Durfee of the Culinary Institute of America; Barbara Fenzl of Les Gourmettes Cooking School; Michelle Gayer of The Salty Tart; Dorie Greenspan; Thomas Gumpel; P. J. Hamel and Jeffrey Hamelman of King Arthur Baking Company; Bill Hanes, Kelly Olson, and Linda Nelson of Red Star Yeast; Kim Harbinson; Molly Herrmann of Kitchen in the Market; Ragavan Iyer (who sat down with Zoë in 2005 and explained how the publishing world really works); Dusti Kugler, Kelly Lainsbury, and Madeline Hill of Food Works; Brenda Langton of Spoonriver restaurant and the Minneapolis Bread Festival; Kevin Masse of The FeedFeed; Tracy Morgan; Silvana Nardone; Stephanie Meyer of FreshTart.com; Riad Nasr, Karl Benson, and Marie Dwyer at Cooks of Crocus Hill; Peter Reinhart; the entire team at Quang; Suvir Saran and Charlie Burd of American Masala; Eliza Woolston Sheffield and Ann Moth of Blue Star Cooking; Tara Steffen of Emile Henry; Jamie Schler; Maria Speck; Joy Summers; and Andrew Zimmern.

Sarah Kieffer has created beautiful content for our website since 2012 and has led us through the crazy world of social media—yet another great way to connect with our readers. Sarah's aesthetic can be seen in her work as our photo and food stylist during the photo shoots for the books. Stephen Gross's photography made all of our breads come to life on the page and depicted the beauty of each recipe.

Graham François (Zoë's husband) created our fabulous website, BreadIn5

.com, and Laura Silver (Jeff's wife) made sure that St. Martin's Press got manuscripts that were already vetted by an experienced editor. And of course, thanks to our kids: Rachel and Julia (Jeff's), and Henri and Charlie (Zoë's), for whom it's been a lifetime of testing and tasting. Our two "little" ones, who fostered our first conversations about bread, are now both college students.

And no acknowledgment would be complete if we didn't thank each other—for being great friends and colleagues for eighteen years.

THE SECRET

~

Mix Enough High-Moisture Dough for Several Loaves and Store It in the Refrigerator

It is so easy to have freshly baked bread when you want it, with only five minutes a day of active effort. First, mix the ingredients into a container all at once, and then let them sit for two hours. Now you are ready to shape and bake the bread, or you can refrigerate the dough and use it over the next couple of weeks. Yes, weeks! Each recipe makes enough dough for many loaves. When you want fresh-baked bread, take a piece of the dough from the container and shape it into a loaf. Let it rest for twenty minutes or more, and then bake. Your house will smell like a bakery and your family and friends will love you for it.

FOREWORD
BY ANDREW ZIMMERN

〜

There is a certain nobility in a "Best of" book. It is implicit. You must have a wealth of material, a rabid fan base, the respect of the industry, the admiration of your peers, and a track record of excellence over a considerable length of time. And you must have given it your all. *Dolly Parton's Greatest Hits* would be a bad joke if she had been a one-hit wonder. Instead, she has several volumes of hits, and for what it's worth, she wrote "Jolene" and "I Will Always Love You" in the same day. She is singular. An only. And that's better than best.

What Zoë and Jeff have done with the **Artisan Bread in Five Minutes** series is prove that the world's easiest yeasted loaf, the most versatile bread dough recipe (even pizza!), can be taken in so many directions and have so many applications that it has created a series of hits, launched a gazillion home bakers on their own bread journey, and spawned, finally, a **Best of Artisan Bread in Five Minutes a Day**, which you are reading right now. This series redefined bread baking for America, long before the Covid-19 sourdough craze. This series of books launched on a simple premise: bread baking can be easy, simple, and anyone can do it. Then it took off—and took on healthy breads, hydration ratios, flatbreads, gluten-free breads, holiday breads, pizza, and more. That's what happens in our culture: Success breeds more success and, in this case, more books.

One of my favorite quotes, and I wish I knew who to attribute it to, says:

There are a lot of rewards for doing good work.
The main reward is the chance to do more good work.
So be sure the work you are doing is the work you want to do.
Because they are going to ask you for more.

And here is a result of doing all that good work: a Best-of book. The contents are superb, the recipes are absolute, the organization and learning gets better with every volume. But I have temporarily been distracted; let me get back to my point. It's always better to be the only than to be the best. To truly celebrate what Jeff and Zoë have accomplished with this milestone edition is to demonstrate their singularity. Best is relative. Only is absolute.

Srini Rao is one of my favorite thinkers, and he put it better than I ever could, "When you're truly unmistakable, the competition becomes completely irrelevant. You're not the best option. You're the only option. When you're the only option, people don't price shop, compare, or wait for what you're selling to go on sale. If you're the only option, people will wait in line to buy your product regardless of what it costs, or in some cases, regardless of what you're selling." That's *Artisan Bread in Five*. And this is their best after proving their only.

Zoë and Jeff didn't set out to conquer the world or to try to beat everyone else. They wanted to spread the gospel of baking bread in a way that everyone could approach in a simple way. They also divined that real and lasting success is playing by rules you make yourself, creating work that either hasn't been done or can't be replicated. Instinctively, they knew it's better to be the only and not the best. And in the end, as you will discover in this book, they've achieved both.

—ANDREW ZIMMERN

1

INTRODUCTION

In early 2020, when pandemic lockdowns sent bread bakers into the kitchen to nourish and comfort loved ones, to rediscover a satisfying creative outlet, or merely to escape from endless days of screens, we began to hear more and more from old friends—our readers. Everyone wanted to tell us about what they were baking and what they were excited to try, and they had lots of questions too, about techniques, equipment, and ingredients. We loved the outpouring of interest. And, of course, we were busy in the kitchen ourselves.

A result of those conversations, this book represents our favorite, most reliably dog-eared recipes from all of our previous books. These are the breads that are staples in our homes, and the recipes our readers ask us about most. We've brought them together here so that anyone looking for a complete bread repertoire will have everything in one place. And those who are newer to this ancient craft have the perfect place to start.

We would give anything to undo the struggle and sadness of the last two years. Yet it's been wonderful to see how bread baking, our beloved pastime, has turned out to be a salve during a worldwide pandemic. Bread has brought us together.

How This Adventure Got Started

It may have been just a little project between friends, but it's become one of the bestselling bread cookbook series of all time, with nearly one million copies in print. It began in our kids' music class in 2003—an unlikely place for coauthors to meet, but in the swirl of toddlers, musical chairs, and xylophones, there was time for the grown-ups to talk. Zoë mentioned that she was a pastry chef and baker who'd been trained at the Culinary Institute of America (CIA). What a happy coincidence—Jeff wasn't a food professional at all; he was a doctor who'd been tinkering for years with an easy, fast method for making homemade bread. He asked her to try a secret recipe he'd been developing, one for which a publisher had already asked for a book proposal. The secret? Mix a big batch of wetter-than-usual dough and store it in the refrigerator. It was promising—everyone loves great bread, and here was a way to make it that was fast, super easy, and cheap (under fifty cents a loaf). But it needed work, so work we did.

We were first-time authors, but we had a publisher who liked our idea and was willing to take a chance on us. Once the thing finally got written and published, we realized our accidental timing was perfect. **Artisan Bread in Five Minutes a Day** came out in 2007, at a moment when technology was rapidly changing how recipes get into the hands of home bakers. We benefited from reviews in *The New York Times*, the Associated Press, regional papers, and web-based news sources—suddenly our ideas were all over the internet.

We were also among the first cookbook authors to maintain an extensive website (BreadIn5.com), where users of our books share ideas and get information that supplements the books. That let us meet a huge community of wonderful home bakers, who were happy to advise us on what recipes to develop next. Our next two books, **Healthy Bread in Five Minutes a Day** (2009) and **Artisan Pizza and Flatbread in Five Minutes a Day** (2011), were based on requests that came from readers, who reached us through the website or social media. Over the years, we've met thousands of bakers just like us—busy people who love fresh bread but don't necessarily have all day to make it. It's been a joy getting to know you all.

Four more books followed: updates of our first two books—*The New Artisan Bread in Five Minutes a Day* (2013) and *The New Healthy Bread in Five Minutes a Day* (2016); then we branched out with *Gluten-Free Bread in Five Minutes a Day* (2016), and *Holiday and Celebration Bread in Five Minutes a Day* (2018), plus translations of our work into German, Chinese, and Japanese, and a version for Great Britain. No one was more surprised than we were to get so many chances to work on so many different types of bread.

Making Artisan Bread in Five Minutes a Day By Refrigerating Pre-Mixed Homemade Yeast Dough

If you've read any of our other books, you know that both of us are obsessed with food—how it tastes and how it's made. We were both bakers: Jeff, a passionate and curious home baker, and Zoë a professional pastry chef. So, while we came to the world of bread cookbook writing through completely different doors, we both wanted the same thing—to spread the word about the delights and simplicity of home-baked bread. That's the Artisan Bread in Five Minutes a Day series.

It seemed to both of us that once upon a time, when we were kids, great traditional bread was available in neighborhood shops all over the United States, but sliced bread (the worst invention ever), in plastic bags, had largely replaced it without anyone noticing. Well, we noticed, and we decided to do something about it. If we couldn't bring back the bakeries, we'd try to bring back the bread. The Artisan Bread in Five Minutes a Day series has been our attempt to help people re-create the great ethnic and American breads of years past, in their own homes, without investing serious time in the process. Using our straightforward, fast, and easy recipes, anyone can create artisan bread and pastries at home with minimal equipment. But who has time to make bread every day?

After years of experimentation, it turns out that we do, and with a method as fast as ours, you can, too. We solved the time problem and produced top-

Visit BreadIn5.com, where you'll find recipes, photos, videos, and instructional material.

quality artisan loaves without a bread machine. We worked out the master recipes during busy years of career transition and starting families. Our lightning-fast
method lets us find the time to bake great bread every day. We developed this
method to recapture the daily artisan-bread experience without further crunch-
ing our limited time—and it works.

Traditional breads made the old-fashioned way need a lot of attention, especially if you want to use a "starter" for that natural, tangy taste. Starters need to
be cared for, with water and flour replenished on a schedule. Dough must be
kneaded until resilient, set to rise, punched down, allowed to rise again. There
are boards and pans and utensils galore to be washed, some of which can't go
into the dishwasher. Very few busy people can go through this every day, if
ever. Even if your friends are all food fanatics, when was the last time you had
homemade bread at a dinner party?

What about bread machines? The machines solve the time problem and
turn out uniformly decent loaves, but, unfortunately, the crust is soft and dull-
flavored, and without tangy flavor in the crumb (the bread's soft interior), unless you use and maintain time-consuming sourdough starter. So we went to
work. We figured out how to subtract complex steps that make the classic technique so time-consuming, and identified a few that can't be omitted. It all came
down to one fortuitous discovery:

Pre-mixed, pre-risen, high-moisture dough keeps well in the refrigerator.

This is the linchpin of our Bread in Five Minutes a Day series. By pre-
mixing high-moisture dough (without kneading) and then storing it, you can
make daily bread baking an easy activity; the only steps you do every day are
shaping and baking. Other books have considered refrigerating dough, but only
for a few days. Still others have omitted the kneading step. But none has tested
the capacity of wet dough to be long-lived in your refrigerator. As our high-

moisture dough ages, it takes on sourdough notes reminiscent of the great European and American natural starters. When dough is mixed with adequate water (this dough is wetter than most you may have worked with), it can be stored in the refrigerator for up to two weeks (enriched or heavy doughs can't go that long but can be frozen instead).

Wetter is better: The wetter dough, as you'll see, is fairly slack and offers less resistance to yeast's expanding carbon dioxide bubbles. So, despite not being replenished with fresh flour and water like a proper sourdough starter, it still has adequate rise, especially in the oven—that's called "oven spring." If you really want to try a true sourdough starter, see our recipe on page 231, which gained in popularity during the pandemic lockdown, when yeast supplies in supermarkets disappeared.

Kneading this kind of dough adds little to the end result; you just don't have to do it. In fact, overhandling stored dough can limit the volume and rise that you get with our method. A one-or two-week supply of dough is made in advance and stored in the refrigerator. Measuring and mixing the large batch of dough takes less than fifteen minutes. Every day, cut off a hunk of dough from the storage container and quickly shape it without kneading. Allow it to rest briefly on the counter and then toss it in the oven. We don't count the rest time (twenty minutes or more depending on the recipe) or baking time (usually about thirty minutes) ·in our five-minutes-a-day calculation, since you can be doing something else while that's happening. If you bake after dinner, the bread will stay fresh for use the next day (higher-moisture breads stay fresh longer), but the method is so convenient that you probably will find you can cut off some dough and bake a loaf every morning before your day starts (especially if you make flatbreads like pita). That, in a nutshell, is how you make artisan breads with only five minutes a day of active effort. **If you want to have one thing you do every day that is simply perfect, this is it.**

Using high-moisture, pre-mixed, pre-risen dough makes most of the difficult, time-consuming, and demanding steps in traditional bread baking completely superfluous:

1. You don't need to make fresh dough every day to have fresh bread every day: Stored high-moisture dough makes wonderful fresh loaves. Only the shaping and baking steps are done daily; the rest has been done in advance.

What we *don't* have to do: steps from traditional artisan baking that we omitted

1. Mix a new batch of dough every time we want to make bread

2. "Proof" yeast

3. Knead dough

4. Rest and rise the loaves in a draft-free location—it doesn't matter

5. Fuss over doubling or tripling of dough volume

6. Punch down and re-rise: **Never** punch down stored dough

7. Poke rising loaves to be sure they've "proofed" by leaving indentations

Now you know why it only takes five minutes a day, not including resting and baking time.

2. You don't absolutely need a "sponge" or "starter": Traditional sourdough recipes require that you keep flour-water mixtures bubbling along in your refrigerator, carefully attended and replenished. But when the dough is stored over two weeks, a subtle sourdough character gradually develops in our breads without the need to maintain sponges or starters in the refrigerator. With our dough-storage approach, your first loaf is not exactly the same as the last because as the dough ages its flavor becomes more complex. Some of our readers like to stagger their batches so they are always baking with dough that has aged at least a few days—we love that strategy. Along the way, we also developed a fast version of traditional sourdough, because some of our readers could not find yeast in the supermarket during the pandemic (see page 231).

3. It doesn't matter how you mix the dry and wet ingredients together: So long as the mixture is uniform, without any dry lumps of flour, it makes no difference whether you use a wooden spoon, a Danish dough whisk (page 36), a heavy-duty stand mixer, or a large-capacity food processor. Choose based on your own convenience and preference.

4. **You don't need to "proof" the yeast:** Traditional recipes require that yeast be dissolved in water with a little sugar and allowed to sit for five minutes to prove that bubbles form and the yeast is alive. But modern yeast simply doesn't fail if used before its expiration date and the baker remembers to use lukewarm, not hot, water. The high water content in our doughs further ensures that the yeast will fully hydrate and activate without a proofing step. Further storage gives it plenty of time to ferment the dough—our approach doesn't need the head start. (Dirty dark secret: If you freeze yeast unopened, or even opened but in an airtight container, it seems to last more or less indefinitely.)

Start a morning batch before work, bake the first loaf before dinner: Here's a convenient way to get fresh bread on the table for dinner. Mix up a full batch of dough before breakfast and store it in the refrigerator. The lukewarm water you used to mix the dough will provide enough heat to allow the yeast to do its thing over the eight hours until you're home. When you walk in the door, cloak and shape the loaf and give it a quick rest, then bake as usual. Small loaves, and especially flatbreads, can be on the table in twenty minutes or less. You can do the same thing with an after-dinner start on the dough—it's ready the next morning.

5. **The dough isn't kneaded:** The dough can be mixed and stored in the same lidded container. No wooden board is required. There should be only one vessel to wash, plus a spoon (or a mixer). You'll never tell the difference between breads made with

kneaded and unkneaded high-moisture dough, so long as you mix it to a basically uniform consistency. In our method, a very quick "cloaking and shaping" step substitutes for kneading (see Step 5 on page 68).

6. **It's hard to over-rise high-moisture stored dough:** Remember that you're storing it anyway. Assuming you start with lukewarm (not cold) water, you'll see a brisk initial rise at room temperature over two hours (don't punch down); then, you'll refrigerate the risen dough for use over the next week or two. But rising longer (even as long as eight hours) won't be harmful; there's lots of leeway in the initial rise time. The exception is dough made with eggs or dairy, which should complete its rising in the refrigerator if it goes beyond two hours (and in the fridge, full rising will take a while).

What's in this "Best-Of..." book? Who is it for?

Wherever you are in the world, we know you were affected by the pandemic. With all of us staying home for safety, those who weren't even interested in home cooking in the "before times" became interested in home-baked bread. In the worst of the lockdown, supermarkets sold out of flour, and even yeast (leading to interest in natural sourdough starter). It led to questions on our website about which of our five books was most useful. That's why we decided to put together a single book of our favorites, including:

- The best of the European and American artisan traditions
- Whole grain loaves
- Pizza and flatbreads
- Brioche, challah, and other sweet or enriched breads
- Gluten-free recipes
- Natural sourdough bread

- New tips, techniques, and shortcuts from BreadIn5.com that never made it into our books, and a few things we never published anywhere

If you only want one of our books, this is the one.

Get started!

With our simple principles and recipes, anyone can make artisan bread at home, and you won't need a professional baker's kitchen. We'll talk about what you'll need to get started in Chapter 2 (Ingredients) and Chapter 3 (Equipment). In Chapter 4, you'll learn the tips and techniques that have taken us years to accumulate. Then, in Chapter 5 (The Master Recipe), we'll lay out the basics of our method, applying them to a variety of simple doughs and variations. Chapter 5's master recipe is the model for the rest of our recipes. We suggest you read it carefully and bake from Chapter 5 first before trying anything else. And if you want more information, we're on the web at BreadIn5.com, where you'll find instructional text, photographs, videos, and a community of other five-minute bakers. Other easy ways to keep in touch: Facebook (@BreadIn5), Instagram (@BreadIn5), Twitter (@ArtisanBreadIn5), Pinterest (@BreadIn5), or on YouTube (@BreadIn5).

As always, our goal remains the same: to help home bakers make great super-fast breads and yeasted sweets but still have a life outside the kitchen. To all of you who helped us make this series happen, thank you! Together we've started a revolution—opening up hundreds of thousands of homes to the satisfaction and delights of homemade bread. But most important, we've had fun, and we hope you do too. After all, if you worry about the bread, it won't taste good.

2

INGREDIENTS

Here's a practical guide to the ingredients we use to produce artisan loaves. Great simple breads can be made with just four ingredients: flour, water, yeast, and salt.

Flours and Grains

All-purpose flour: All-purpose flour is our number-one choice for white flour because most households have it in the pantry and it has medium (rather than high) protein content. Most of the protein in wheat is highly elastic gluten, which allows bread dough to trap the carbon dioxide gas produced by yeast. Without gluten, bread wouldn't rise. That's why flours containing only minimal gluten (like rye) need to be mixed with wheat flour to make a successful loaf. Traditional bread recipes stress the need to develop gluten through kneading, which turns out not to be an important factor if you keep the dough wet.

With a protein content of about 10 percent in most national brands, all-purpose flour will have adequate gluten to create a satisfying "chew," but not so much protein as to cause heaviness. Gluten is strengthened when the proteins align themselves into strands after water is added. This creates a network that traps gas bubbles and creates an airy interior crumb. These lined-up strands can be formed in two ways:

- **By kneading:** Not the way we like to spend our time. **OR** . . .
- **By using lots of water:** The gluten strands become mobile enough to *align themselves.*

Creating a wet dough is the basis for our no-knead method. It's easy to consistently achieve this moisture level with U.S.-grown all-purpose flour. We tested our recipes with standard supermarket all-purpose flours. **Some all-purpose white flours have more protein and need extra water.** These flours have a protein content of about 11.5 percent:

- King Arthur Unbleached All-Purpose Flour
- Dakota Maid Unbleached All-Purpose Flour
- Most Canadian all-purpose flours

They work well in our recipes, but if you use them, you need to increase the water a little—in the Master Recipe (page 63), use about ¼ cup extra water—or the dough will be drier than usual. And some flours have *too little* protein to make successful high-moisture dough—stay away from cake flour and pastry flours (around 8 percent protein).

We prefer unbleached flours for their natural creamy color, and our preference to avoid unnecessary chemicals (but modern bleached flour absorbs water just the same as unbleached, and doesn't require any recipe changes).

Bread flour: Bread flour is a white flour with about 12 percent protein. If you prefer extra-chewy bread, you can substitute bread flour for all-purpose by increasing the water by ⅓ cup in the Master Recipe (page 63). For specialty breads that are nicer when they can hold a particular shape during resting, like *pain d'épi* (page 92), bagels (page 146), and pretzels (page 150), we call for the option to use bread flour without ad-justing the water (see Strong White Dough, page 77).

Whole wheat flour: Whole wheat flour contains both the germ and bran of wheat, both of which are healthful and tasty. Together they add a slightly bitter, nutty flavor to bread that most people enjoy. The naturally occurring oils in wheat germ prevent formation of a crackling crust, so you're going for a different type of loaf when you start increasing the proportion of whole wheat flour. In general, you can use any kind of whole wheat flour that's available to you. Stone-ground whole wheat flour will be a bit coarser, denser, and more rustic, and it may require a little more water than what we call for—we tested with non-stone-ground supermarket whole wheat flour. Whole wheat pastry flour is very low in protein but it works fine when mixed with white flour.

> ͡ʘ
>
> **Storing whole wheat flour:** Oils in whole wheat flour can go rancid if stored for long periods at room temperature. So if you don't use it often, store it in an airtight container in the freezer (the container needs to be really, really airtight).

White whole wheat flour: White whole wheat flour is 100 percent whole grain, but it's ground from a light-colored wheat berry rather than the usual "red" (dark brown) one. It's pale-colored and milder tasting, but it packs the same nutrition as regular whole wheat. It measures and absorbs water just like regular whole wheat and can be used as a substitute for it. Don't expect it to taste like white flour and don't try to substitute it 1:1 for all-purpose or you'll get a dry, dense dough that won't store well at all—whole grain dough requires more water.

Vital wheat gluten (sometimes called "vital wheat gluten flour"): You can boost dough "strength" (and the bread's protein level) by using this powdered extract of wheat's endosperm, and many of our readers preferred whole grain loaves when they had this extra gluten boost. So, why increase the gluten in whole grain bread?

Visit BreadIn5.com, where you'll find recipes, photos, videos, and instructional material.

In whole wheat flours, the nutritious bran and germ are ground into the flour and take the place of some of the gluten-rich endosperm (the white part of the wheat kernel). So, whole wheat flour has significantly less gluten than white flour, and this will mean less rising power and a less "open" airy crumb (the interior of the bread). What's worse is that whole wheat's bran particles have sharp edges that cut and disrupt developing gluten strands. So breads made with 100 percent whole wheat flour tend to be denser than white breads, especially when made from stored dough. Extra gluten can help counter that and promote an airier whole grain result, with a stronger protein network that traps more gas. You don't have to use it, but many of our testers preferred the more structured, higher-rising loaf that you get with vital wheat gluten (see 100% Whole Wheat Dough on page 79 for instructions on making whole grain doughs with and without vital wheat gluten).

Two brands of vital wheat gluten are widely available in U.S. supermarkets: Bob's Red Mill and Hodgson Mill. King Arthur Baking Company also has one available online or through mail order. Vital wheat gluten is easy to incorporate into recipes but can form firm lumps in dough if not handled properly. To prevent that, **always whisk vital wheat gluten with the dry ingredients before adding liquids.** Vital wheat gluten should be refrigerated in an airtight container once opened.

Some of our whole grain recipes, especially when there are other heavy ingredients like fruit in them, do better with vital wheat gluten. These recipes still work without it, but if you omit the vital wheat gluten you'll need to decrease the liquid—by about ½ cup in a full-batch recipe.

Rye flour: Specialty catalogs offer a bewildering variety of rye flours, including "medium" rye (low bran) and dark rye (higher bran), plus very coarsely ground rye meal (sometimes labeled as pumpernickel or whole grain rye flour, depending on how coarsely it is ground).

The flours have varying percentages of rye bran, but the labeling generally doesn't make this clear. Be aware, though, that the very coarse-ground high-bran products will produce a coarser, denser loaf when used in our method.

You will not be able to get too particular about this ingredient, because in U.S. supermarkets, choices are usually limited to high-bran, high-protein varieties like Hodgson Mill Stone-Ground Whole Grain Rye and Bob's Red Mill Organic Stone-Ground Rye Flour. "Medium" rye, with reduced bran and protein, is available from King Arthur Baking Company (see Sources for Bread-Baking Products, page 243), and it produces a rye loaf that's closer to commercial rye bread. Whichever kind of rye you use, it must be paired with wheat flour because it's low in gluten and won't rise well on its own. Use the various rye products interchangeably in our recipes, based on your taste.

Organic flours: We don't detect flavor or texture differences with organic flour, but if you like organic products, by all means use them (we often do). They're not required, and they certainly cost more. That said, home-baked bread made with organic flour is way less expensive than commercial organic bread. A few brands of organic flour are available in the supermarket, but the best selection is at your local organic food co-op, where you can buy it in bulk.

Gluten-Free Flours for People Who Don't Eat Wheat

If you have celiac disease or are allergic to or intolerant of gluten, double-check with your doctor before consuming any new grain. We tested our gluten-free recipes with Bob's Red Mill brand flours. If you make brand substitutions, you'll have to experiment with the amounts and proportions because brands vary widely in the amount of water they absorb. If you absolutely can't tolerate gluten, check your yeast label, because some are made with dough enhancers that contain enzymes derived from wheat. These flours are meant for the gluten-free breads on pages 173–82 and cannot be used as a substitute for wheat flours in any of the other recipes.

Brown rice flour: Brown rice flour is made from rice with its external bran left in place and ground into the final product. It's higher in nutrients and fiber than white rice flour. Since our recipes also call for substantial amounts of other white gluten-free flours, we prefer brown rice flour over white, and swapping them will result in major changes in the amount of water needed in the recipe.

Sorghum flour: Sorghum is a very popular cooking grain related to sugarcane. It is used around the world but has just recently found its way into American kitchens.

Tapioca flour/tapioca starch: Tapioca is made from a root that's known by many names: cassava, manioc, or yucca. It is extracted and ground into a flour that is high in starch, calcium, and vitamin C, but low in protein. It is most often associated with its thickening properties, but it is now frequently used in gluten-free baking. It is sold as both tapioca starch and tapioca flour, but they are exactly the same.

Teff flour: An indispensable grain in Ethiopia, teff had been virtually unheard of in the rest of the world until recently. It is a variety of whole grain millet that is wonderfully sweet but packed with iron and calcium, and in gluten-free loaves it tastes something like rye.

Cornmeal and cornstarch: Cornmeal is just the whole, de-hulled corn kernel, ground coarsely into a "meal"; it makes a great base for sliding loaves off a peel. Degerminated cornmeal has had its nutritious "germ" removed, but it has better shelf life at room temperature, so many commercial cornmeals are sold that way. Cornstarch is a different animal—it's a refined product that has neither the bran nor the germ—just the starch. It creates a smooth texture and acts as a binder in gluten-free dough.

Gluten-Free Ingredients for Adding Structure

Either xanthan gum or psyllium husk creates gas-trapping structure, stretchiness, and chew in gluten-free dough. They're needed to replace some of the properties of gluten, and gluten-free breads won't work without one of them. They're interchangeable in the gluten-free recipes in this book. The food additive **xanthan gum** has long been used as a thickener in commercial food products. It is refined from a bacterial fermentation process that begins with natural sugars—the bacteria create the final starch-like compound. **Ground psyllium husk**, sometimes sold as "powdered" psyllium husk, is a more naturally derived product. Like xanthan gum, it produces gas-trapping structure, but it's a plant-based fiber supplement, milled from the outer coating of an edible seed, that's available at pharmacies, food co-ops, or online.

Water

Throughout the book we call for lukewarm water. This means water that feels just a little warm to the touch; if you measured it with a thermometer it would be no higher than 100°F (38°C). The truth is, we never use a thermometer and we've never had a yeast failure due to excessive temperature—but it can happen, so be careful. Cold tap water will work (and you cannot kill yeast with cold water) but the initial rise will take much, much longer (the bread will be just as good, and some tasters even prefer the taste of cold-risen dough). Typically, in our homes, we're in no hurry, so we often use cold water and let it sit for eight hours or more (refrigerate egg-enriched dough to complete its rising after two hours at room temperature).

About water sources: We find that the flavors of wheat and yeast overwhelm the contribution of water to bread's flavor, so we use ordinary tap water run through a home water filter, but that's only because it's what we drink at home. Assuming your own tap water tastes good enough to drink, use it filtered or unfiltered; we can't tell the difference in finished bread. The only place we highly recommend filtered water is when creating sourdough starter, since some tap water is highly chlorinated and can affect the growth of natural yeasts.

Visit BreadIn5.com, where you'll find recipes, photos, videos, and instructional material.

Yeast: Adjust the Amount to Your Taste and Patience

Use whatever yeast is readily available; with our approach you won't be able to tell the difference between the various national brands of granulated yeast (though we tested our recipes with the Red Star brand), nor between packages labeled "active dry," "instant," "quick-rise," or "bread-machine." All generally available yeast products are granulated, which means they are dried to a very coarse powder and will dissolve readily once in contact with water or wet dough.

There's one product that isn't granulated: fresh cake yeast. It's a very traditional product that works fine in our recipes (though you will have to increase the yeast volume by 50 percent to achieve the same rising speed). Manufacturers date it for a short expiration time, and it needs careful preparation to dissolve before use. Since we don't find that it delivers superior flavor and is hard to find, we don't generally recommend it.

The long storage time of our doughs acts as an equalizer between all of those subtly different yeast products. After several days of high-moisture storage, yeasted dough begins to take on a flavor and aroma that's close to the flavor of natural sourdough starters used in many artisan breads. This will deepen the flavor and character of all your doughs. The traditional way to achieve these flavors—pre-ferments, sours, and starters like *biga* (Italian), *levain* (French), and *poolish* (eastern European)—all require significant time

> **Using yeast packets instead of jarred or bulk yeast:** Throughout the book, we call for 1 tablespoon of granulated yeast for about 4 pounds of dough. **You can substitute one packet of granulated yeast for a tablespoon, even though, technically speaking, those amounts aren't perfectly equivalent (1 tablespoon is a little more than the 2¼ teaspoons found in one packet).** We've found that this makes little difference in the initial rise time or in the performance of the finished dough.

and attention. Our method provides the flavor without all that effort.

One strong recommendation: If you bake frequently, buy yeast in **bulk or in 4-ounce jars, rather than in packets (which are much less economical).** Food co-ops often sell yeast by the pound, in bulk (usually the Red Star brand). Make sure that bulk-purchased yeast is fresh by chatting with your co-op manager. Freeze yeast after opening to extend its shelf life and use it straight from the freezer, or store smaller containers in the refrigerator and use within a few months. Between the two of us, we've had only one yeast failure in many years of baking, and it was with an outdated envelope stored at room temperature. **The key to avoiding yeast failure is to use water that is no warmer than lukewarm (about 100°F). Hot water kills yeast.**

Will the recipes work with small amounts of yeast? Some readers prefer less yeast in their dough—finding that a long, slow rise produces a better flavor—but it's really a matter of taste. Less yeast works well for all of our recipes except for the gluten-free dough—but the initial rise will be slower. This book uses less yeast than our very first edition of *Artisan Bread in Five Minutes a Day* from 2007—but you can go even lower if you have time to spare. We've had great results using as little as one-quarter of our standard amount of yeast. If you decrease the yeast, the initial rising time may increase to eight hours, or even longer, depending on how much you decreased it and the temperature in your house.

Slowing things down with cold water: Another way to slow down the rise and build flavor is to start with cool or even cold water. If you try this, the initial rise time increases dramatically, even more so if you also decreased the

Modern yeast almost never fails if used before its expiration date, so you do not need to "proof" the yeast (i.e., test it for freshness by demonstrating that it bubbles in sweetened warm water). And you don't have to wait for yeast to fully dissolve after mixing with water. You can even mix all the dry ingredients first, including the yeast, and then add the liquids.

yeast, so you'll need more advance planning. **If you're making dough with eggs and you're considering a long, slow rise, do only the first two hours at room temperature,** then transfer to the refrigerator to complete the rise (and expect a long wait). According to the U.S. Department of Agriculture, raw eggs shouldn't be kept at room temperature for longer than two hours.*

Salt: Adjust It to Your Taste

All of our recipes were tested with Morton brand kosher salt, which is coarsely ground. We call for kosher salt because it's a cheap, consistent form of neutral-tasting salt that's easy to measure and cook with. Any coarse salt will work in our recipes. If you measure salt by volume and you're using something finer or coarser than the Morton brand, you need to adjust the amount, because finer salt packs denser in the spoon. The following measurements are equivalent:

- **Table salt (fine):** 2 teaspoons
- **Morton Kosher Salt (coarse):** 1 tablespoon
- **Diamond Kosher Salt (coarsest):** 1 tablespoon plus 1 teaspoon

You can use sea salt, but be sure to adjust for its grind. If it's finely ground, you need to measure it like table salt above, and if it's more coarsely ground than Morton, you'll need to increase the volume accordingly. And reserve the really expensive artisan sea salts for sprinkling on finished products—artisan salts lose their unique flavors when baked.

In traditional bread recipes, salt is used not only for flavor—it also helps tighten and strengthen the gluten. Because our dough is slack in the first place, and is stored for so long, the differences between high- and low-salt versions of

---

* U.S. Department of Agriculture Fact Sheet. Egg Products Preparation: Shell Eggs from Farm to Table. https://www.fsis.usda.gov/food-safety/safe-food-handling-and-preparation/eggs/shell-eggs-farm-table. Accessed June 1, 2021.

our doughs are less pronounced. Adjust the salt to suit your palate and your health—we give you a range. We love the taste of salt and don't have any health-related salt restrictions, so we tend to use the higher amounts. Saltier dough can help bring out flavor early in the batch-life, but if you like our doughs best after they've been stored awhile, you may find you can decrease the salt. The low end of our salt range will be salty enough for many—and if health conditions require it, you can decrease the salt radically and the recipes will still work. In fact, you can bring the salt all the way down to zero, though the taste and texture will certainly change.

Weighing yeast and salt: We provide weight equivalents for yeast and salt, which is a more professional technique **and avoids the problem of compensating for fineness of grind**. But professionals measure out enormous batches. For typical home batches, be sure your home scale weighs accurately in the lower ranges; otherwise spoon-measure yeast and salt.

Enrichment: Butter, Oils, and Eggs

When people first taste homemade artisan bread, they're sure that the moisture and flavor must be coming from butter, fats, or eggs. For our basic breads, they're wrong; the moisture comes from—you guessed it—moisture, the high level of water in our dough. But for some of our breads, like the challahs and brioches in Chapter 11, fats and oils are important components of the flavor and texture.

Butter: Butter is delicious and is a staple in rich, festive breads. There is no substitute for it in brioche (page 195). We tested with national brands, but if you can find locally made butter, by all means use it. We always call for unsalted butter so that you can control the saltiness of your recipe.

Vegetable oils: Blends, or pure oils made from soybeans, safflower, sunflower, peanuts, canola, grapeseed, or corn, all work interchangeably in our recipes that call for oil. Neutral-flavored oils don't impart noticeable flavor to baked breads. Others work just as well in our recipes but impart desirably distinctive flavors:

Olive oil: It's one of the most delightful flavors in Western cooking—there's nothing like it (except maybe olives). If you like its flavor as much as we do, you can use it in any of our recipes that call for oil. It's central to the flavors in many of our Mediterranean-inspired pizzas, flatbreads, and bread sticks. You can use either regular or extra-virgin olive oil in our recipes, but extra-virgin is the most flavorful.

Avocado oil: Avocado oil imparts a hint of delicious avocado flavor.

Flaxseed oil: Flaxseed oil has a neutral flavor in recipes calling for up to a half-cup in a four-pound batch of dough. This is a super-healthy oil, and according to the Flax Council of Canada, it's stable at baking temperatures, but it must be refrigerated or it can go rancid—and that's when it can impart a strong flavor, and it isn't pleasant. Think of fish-flavored bread.

Coconut oil: Coconut oil is solid at room temperature, so melt it in a microwave on low or in a double boiler before using in recipes calling for liquid oil. It imparts a mild coconut flavor.

Eggs: All our recipes were tested with large eggs. They should be at room temperature before adding to recipes, or they will chill the dough, necessitating a longer rising time. If your eggs aren't at room temperature, put them (unshelled) in a bowl of warm water (you should still be comfortable touching it) for ten minutes. See the note on page 20 about safe handling of eggs, especially if you're decreasing the yeast in the recipes. If you want to try an egg substitute, make a small dough-batch to see if you like it before you commit.

Seeds and Nuts

Seeds define the flavor of some breads; caraway seeds are so central to the flavor of some rye breads (page 122) that a lot of people think that caraway is actually the flavor of the rye grain. (It's not, but for us, something does seem to be missing in unseeded rye bread.) The only problem you can run into with caraway, sesame, poppy, or other seeds is that their oils can go rancid if you store the seeds too long. Taste a few if your jar is older than a year, and freeze if you plan to store them for longer than three months. The same goes for nuts—they can go bad too, so taste before using.

Unconventional seeds: If you're feeling adventurous, replace traditional seeds like caraway, sesame, or poppy with anise, fennel, crushed coriander, or even cumin seeds. If you're hesitant about these strong flavors, just use them as a topping for a section of a loaf and see what you think. If you're pleased with the flavor, you can add seeds right in the dough for your next loaf.

Sweeteners

White granulated: This is the most common form, providing pure, white sweetness. Our recipes work equally well with cane or beet sugars, the two main varieties found in the United States. Sugar also tenderizes baked breads, and helps them retain moisture, so if your loaves seem dry, a couple of tablespoons of sugar, honey, or barley malt in a four-pound batch can help.

Brown sugar and raw sugar: Like white sugar, these less refined sugars are made from sugarcane or sugar beets, but they retain trace amounts of the nutrients found in molasses. Brown sugar can be light or dark, and for our purposes it doesn't matter which one you pick. The color of the brown sugar is determined by how much molasses is added back to the white sugar before packaging. These sugars impart a caramel flavor as well. If you bake with cup measures, be sure to pack the brown sugar into the cup to get the accurate amount. Raw sugars are most commonly found as demerara, muscovado, and turbinado, and have a larger grain than regular brown sugar.

Confectioners' (powdered) sugar: This fine, powdery sugar is generally only used to dust over a bread or in icing recipes for the top of a loaf—we don't bake with it. Raw sugar is also only used on the top of the loaf. Its larger grains don't mix into the dough quite as well, and it measures differently because of the size of the crystals. You can use standard or organic brands for any of the recipes. We did not test coconut sugar or other sugar sources for these recipes, so you will need to experiment with their sweetness intensity.

Liquid sweeteners: These impart flavor when used in place of granulated sugar:

- **Honey:** Produced by busy bees the world over from naturally occurring sugars in the nectar of the flowers they visit, honey is the liquid sweetener we call for most frequently in our sweetened or enriched recipes. Honey's flavor is determined by the type of plant nectar the honeybee collects. Some honeys have intense flavor, such as buckwheat honey, while others are quite mild, such as clover honey. We've had great results with all kinds of honey, so experiment with different ones and see which you prefer.
- **Barley malt (malt syrup):** Made from sprouted barley, it is very dark, sweet with malt sugar, and quite thick. It adds a beery, yeasty flavor to bread. Barley malt is the main ingredient in beer, and malt sugar is a great sugar for feeding yeast.

Stevia: Some of our readers, especially diabetics or prediabetics who avoid sugar, asked us about this herbal sweetener. Stevia sweetens without sugar, but it's not an artificial chemical—it's an extract of a South American herb whose leaves contain a naturally occurring, zero-calorie substance that is much sweeter-tasting than sugar. There are two kinds of stevia products: pure ones (liquid or powder), and those combined with other substances—starch or sugar-derived additives like erythritol or maltodextrin—so they measure and look like sugar. If you use the pure stevia products, you only need to use a small amount—it has much more concentrated sweetening power. The labeling will tell you the volume equivalency to sugar (and sugar is about equivalent in sweetening power to honey, by volume). There's some controversy about the additives in the mixed commercial stevia products designed to measure like sugar. The question is whether these substances are prone to raise blood sugar. Most experts suggest that diabetics can consume these additives in modest quantity. Read the label, check with your health provider, and use your best judgment. If you want to be extra careful, avoid the products that include any additives and stick with pure stevia powders or liquids. Our favorite product is a pure liquid extract, and it works well as a swap for sugar or honey in 4- to 5-pound batches of challah that's ordinarily sweetened with sugar or honey—full recipes require twenty drops of the liquid. That's how concentrated liquid stevia is. You can experiment with stevia in place of sugar, honey, or other sweeteners, or at least as a way to decrease the sugar in a recipe. It doesn't taste exactly the same, but many people find it to be a natural product that makes a nice substitute.

3

EQUIPMENT

We've tried to keep our list spare, and present items in order of importance. You can make a successful bread with your old, thin cookie sheets, you can skip the baking stone, and you don't need to buy the specialized dough-storage containers if you don't want to—especially when you're just starting out. That said, the most helpful items are the following:

- Equipment for baking with steam: we'll give you four options
- Baking stone, baking steel, cast-iron pizza pan, cast-iron skillet, or unglazed quarry tiles
- Oven thermometer
- Pizza peel

See Sources for Bread-Baking Products (page 243) to locate mail-order and web-based vendors for harder-to-find items.

Equipment for Baking with Steam
(You Only Need One of These)

Easiest option is a metal broiler tray or aluminum pan to catch water to create steam: This is our first choice for creating the steam needed for lean-dough breads—those made without fat or eggs—to achieve a crispy crust. (Enriched breads like challah and brioche don't benefit from baking with steam because the fat in the dough softens the crust.) Pour hot water (or drop a handful of ice cubes) into the preheated metal broiler tray just before closing the oven door.

Some ovens (including many professional-style ones and many that heat with gas) don't have a good seal for holding in steam. *If your oven allows steam to dissipate and you're not getting a great crust with the broiler-tray method, try one of these three alternatives:*

Two important warnings:

1. Do not use a glass pan to catch water for steam, or it will shatter on contact with the water.

2. We've gotten rare reports of cracked oven-window glass from water accidentally spilled on the hot glass, mostly with older ovens that didn't have tempered glass. If you want extra assurance that this won't happen, cover the window with a towel before pouring water into the tray and remove before closing the oven door.

---

1. **Food-grade spray bottle:** Spray the loaf with water before closing the oven door, then open it at 30-second intervals for two more sprayings.

2. **Metal bowl or aluminum-foil roasting pan for covering free-form loaves in the oven:** By trapping steam next to the loaf as it bakes, you can create the humid environment that produces a crisp crust without using a broiler tray or a sprayer. The bowl or dish needs to be heat tolerant and tall enough so that the rising loaf won't touch it, but not

so large that it extends beyond the edge of the stone; otherwise, it won't trap the steam.

3. **Clay baker, covered cast-iron pot, or inverted loaf pan:** The clay baker (in French, *la cloche* [la klōsh], meaning "bell," after its distinctive shape) is a time-honored way to bake—the covered, unglazed-clay baking vessel traps steam inside, so the crackling crust forms without the need for a baking stone, broiler tray, water, or sprayer. Crispiest results are obtained with a twenty- to thirty-minute preheat. We don't soak clay bakers in water before use as is sometimes advocated, and unglazed clay shouldn't be greased. It's easiest (but not required) to rest the loaf on parchment paper, and then carefully slide the loaf, paper and all, into the preheated baker when ready to bake. Start the baking with the cover on, but finish baking uncovered for the last third of the baking time. Covered cast-iron pots also work well when used this same way, though some of them will need a heat-resistant replacement knob—check with the manufacturer. And if you're making bread in a loaf pan, and you have two identical pans, you can invert one on top of the other to create the steam environment.

Other Equipment

Baking stone, cast-iron pizza pan, baking steel, cast-iron skillet, or unglazed quarry tiles: Bread turns out browner, crisper, and tastier when the dough is baked on one of these, especially in combination with a steam environment (see page 28). Products may be labeled "pizza stones" (usually round), or "baking stones" (usually rectangular). The larger rectangular ones (14 × 16 inches) will keep flour, cornmeal, and other ingredients from falling to the oven floor. In our experience, ceramic stones are durable but don't last forever, especially the thinner ones—we no longer find any manufacturers willing to guarantee them against cracking. Thick stones take longer to preheat compared to thinner ones, or to cast-iron (see below), but in general, are more resistant to cracking. The metal options (cast-iron and steel) work great and do not ever crack, in our experience.

Unglazed quarry tiles, available from home-improvement stores, are inexpensive and work well. The drawbacks: You'll need several of them to line an

oven rack, and stray cornmeal or flour may fall between the tiles onto the oven floor, where it will burn.

Traditionally, professionals have given two reasons to bake right on a ceramic stone. **First,** the stone promotes fast and even heat transfer because of its weight and density (versus, for example, a baking sheet), so it quickly dries and crisps the crust. That massive heat transfer also promotes "oven spring," especially in home ovens that don't deliver even heat. "Oven spring" is the sudden expansion of gases within the bread—it occurs upon contact with the hot air and stone, and it prevents a dense, tough result. **Second,** it's always been assumed that the stone's porosity allows it to absorb excess moisture from the dough (especially wet dough), encouraging crispness. It turns out that the effect must be mostly due to explanation number one, because we've found that dough baked on preheated cast-iron pizza pans, baking steels, and even in preheated cast-iron skillets, turns out as well as dough baked on stones, despite the fact that metal isn't porous at all.

Having said all this, we must emphasize that you can make decent bread without a baking stone; a heavy-gauge baking sheet (see page 33) is a good second choice. The crust won't be as crisp, but the result will be better than most any bread you can buy. And stones aren't required for loaves baked in a loaf pan.

Pizza peel: This is a flat board with a long handle used to slide bread or pizza onto a hot stone. Wood or metal work well, but don't use anything made of plastic to transfer dough onto a stone—it could melt upon contact. Prepare the peel with cornmeal, flour, or parchment paper before putting dough on it, or everything will stick to it, and possibly to your stone. If you don't have a pizza peel, a flat baking sheet without sides (rimless) will do, but it will be more difficult to handle. A thin wood cutting board also works in a pinch—some have handles that make them almost as easy to work with as peels.

Oven thermometer: Home ovens are often off by up to 75 degrees, so this is an important item. You need to know the actual oven temperature to get predictable bread-baking results. An inexpensive oven thermometer (less than twenty dollars) will help you get results just like the ones you see in our photos. Place your oven thermometer right on the stone for best results.

A hot oven drives excess water out of wet dough, but if it's too hot you'll burn the crust before fully baking the crumb (the bread's interior). Too low, and you'll end up with a pale crust and undercooked crumb unless you extend the baking time—but that can give you a thick, tough crust. Without the thermometer, your bread baking will have an annoying element of trial and error. If your oven runs significantly hot or cool, you may want to have it recalibrated by a professional. Otherwise, compensate by adjusting the heat setting to reach the desired thermometer reading. When a baking stone is in place, your oven may take longer to reach final temperature than the twenty or thirty-minute preheat that we specify. And digital oven settings are no more accurate than old-fashioned dial displays, so rely on your oven thermometer. If you don't like the result you're getting with a short preheat, consider a longer one (forty-five or even sixty minutes).

Bucket; large plastic storage container; or glass, stainless-steel, or crockery container or pot with a lid: You can mix and store the dough in the same vessel—this will save you from washing one more item (it all figures into the five minutes a day). Look for a food-grade container that holds about 6 quarts, to allow for the initial rise. Round containers are easier to mix in than square ones (flour gets caught in corners). Great options are available on our website or

from kitchen-supply stores or discount chains. Some food-storage buckets include a vented lid, which allows gases to escape during the fermentation process. Another vented option is a beer fermentation bucket, which is sold at beer-making (home-brew) stores. You can usually close the vent (or seal the lid) after the first two days because gas production has really slowed by then. If your vessel has a plastic lid, you can poke a tiny hole in the lid to allow gas to escape.

Avoid glass or crockery containers that create a truly airtight seal (with a screw top, for example), because trapped gases could shatter them (see photo).

If you don't have a vented container, just leave the lid open a crack for the first two days of storage. And of course, you can always use a mixing bowl covered with plastic wrap, or a soup kettle with a lid (don't cover dough with a towel—that works for traditional dough, but it will stick horribly to this high-moisture dough).

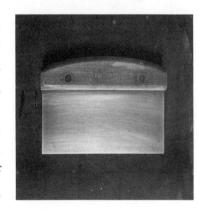

Dough scraper ("bench knife"): A dough scraper makes it easier to work with wet dough—especially when you're just starting out. It can help lessen the temptation to work in extra flour to prevent things from sticking to the work surface. Just scrape wet dough off the work surface when it sticks—this is particularly useful when working with dough as it's rolled out for pizza or flatbread. Steel scrapers are handy for clearing excess cornmeal or flour off your hot baking stone. The flexible plastic ones are also great, but not on hot surfaces. They're preferred when your work surface scratches easily, or for scraping dough out of bowls or containers, where they conform flexibly to the surface.

Heavy-gauge rimmed baking sheet, jelly-roll pan, or cookie sheet: The highest-quality baking sheets are made of heavyweight aluminum and have short rims (sometimes called jelly-roll pans). When well greased or lined with parchment paper or a silicone mat, they are a decent alternative to the pizza peel/baking stone method and let you avoid sliding dough off a pizza peel onto a stone. Similar-gauge flat, round pans are available specifically for pizza. Avoid "air in-sulated" baking sheets—they don't conduct heat well and won't produce a crisp crust. Thin cookie sheets can be used but, like air-insulated bakeware, they won't produce a great crust and can scorch bottom crusts due to their uneven heat delivery.

Silicone mats: Nonstick, flexible silicone baking mats are convenient and can be reused thousands of times. They're terrific for lower-temperature recipes such as sweet brioches and challahs, but we find that lean doughs don't crisp as well on silicone. They're used on top of a baking sheet or dropped onto a hot stone and don't need to be greased, so cleanup is a breeze. Be sure to get a mat rated to the temperature you need—some brands aren't rated for high-temperature baking.

Baguette pan (metal or silicone): We usually bake French baguettes right on a stone, but a metal or silicone baguette pan works as an alternative. These pans are a great way to bake several beautifully shaped baguettes at once, without crowding. They also prevent sideways spreading, which can give baguettes an odd shape when using longer-aged or wetter dough. If using a metal pan, line it with parchment to prevent the bread from sticking.

Parchment paper: Parchment paper is an alternative to flour or cornmeal for preventing dough from sticking to the pizza peel as it's slid into the oven. Use a paper that's temperature-rated to withstand what's called for in your recipe. The paper goes along with the loaf, right onto the preheated stone, and can be removed halfway through baking to crisp up the bottom crust. Parchment paper can also be used to line baking sheets, and this can substitute for greasing the sheet. Don't use products labeled as pastry parchment, butcher paper, or waxed paper—they will smoke and stick miserably to baked bread dough.

Loaf pans: For sandwich loaves, we prefer smaller pans with approximate dimensions of 8½ × 4½ inches. With high-moisture dough, it can be difficult to get bigger loaves to bake through. This size pan is sometimes labeled as holding 1 pound of dough, but we specify a more generous fill for taller slices—up to 2 pounds when filled three-quarters full. Like baking sheets and silicone mats, loaf pans work well but don't promote the development of a crisp and beautifully colored crust—wherever the pan touches the bread, it's going to be pale compared to free-form loaves. Some of our readers have preferred pans with a nonstick coating with our wet doughs, which tend to stick, and even for nonstick, we recommend greasing the pan. But as we've experimented more and more, we've found that well-greased, uncoated aluminum pans, or glazed ceramic pans release just fine. The trick is to allow the fully baked loaf to sit in its pan at room temperature for ten minutes after baking. The loaf then "steams" itself out of adherence to the pan and you can coax it out by running a table knife around the loaf and then prying it out with a wide spatula. Turn loaf breads with the flat side up for slicing (see sidebar, page 87).

Brioche pans: Traditionally, brioche is baked either in a fluted brioche mold or in a loaf pan. The fluted mold is easy to find either online or in any baking supply store. They are available in several sizes, with or without a nonstick coating. Flexible silicone brioche molds are also available.

Mini loaf pans: For smaller sandwich breads, and especially when baking with kids, it's fun to use mini loaf pans. They're sometimes labeled "number-1" loaf pans, measure about 6 × 3 inches, and hold about three-quarters of a pound of dough. The loaves bake faster than those in full-size loaf pans, so check for doneness sooner than the recipe calls for when using them.

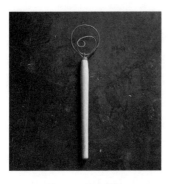

Dough whisk, sometimes called "Danish" dough whisk: Unlike flimsy egg-beating whisks, Danish-style dough whisks are made from strong non-bendable wire on a wood handle, and they're used to blend liquid and dry ingredients together quickly in the dough bucket. We find that they work faster and offer less resistance than a traditional wooden spoon—though a wooden spoon works fine.

Rolling pin: You'll need one if you want to make any of our rolled-out desserts, and using one definitely speeds up the process of flattening dough for pizzas. We love the skinny French rolling pins that look like large dowels, tapered or straight, but traditional American-style pins with handles work well, too. We have tried them all and find that wood, marble, and metal all get the job done; we've even rolled out the dough with a bottle of wine in a pinch.

Bread knife: A serrated bread knife does a great job cutting through fresh bread without tearing or compressing it. It's also the best implement we've found for slashing high-moisture loaves just before baking. Razor blades and French lames (lămm), usually recommended in traditional artisan baking methods, catch and stick in very wet dough (especially for beginners)—not so for serrated bread knives.

Cooling rack: This is fashioned of wire or other thin metal and is usually intended for cake. It's very helpful in preventing the soggy bottom crust that can result when you cool bread on a plate or other nonporous surface.

Measuring spoons: Seek out a set that includes a ½-tablespoon measure in addition to the usual suspects. Some of our ingredient lists call for ½ tablespoons. If you can't find a measuring set with a ½-tablespoon measure, just measure out 1½ teaspoons.

Measuring cups: Avoid 2-cup measuring cups because they are inaccurate when used with the scoop-and-sweep method specified in our recipes, collecting too much flour due to excessive packing down into the cup. And be sure to use *dry* measuring cups for flour, which allow you to level the top of the cup by sweeping across with a knife; you can't level off a liquid measuring cup filled with flour. Measuring cups become largely unnecessary if you use a scale to measure in flour. . . .

Scale: We love to weigh our ingredients rather than use measuring cups, because it's faster and more accurate. Digital scales are getting cheaper all the time, so we now include weights for ingredients in all our dough recipes. Just press "tare" or "zero" after each ingredient is added to the dough vessel and the scale does the arithmetic for you (see page 41).

The scale is also a consistent way to measure out dough for loaves or flatbreads, but it isn't absolutely necessary because we also give you a visual cue for dough weight (for example, a grapefruit-size piece is 1 pound, and an orange-size piece is about ½ pound of dough).

Serrated steak knife, kitchen shears: You'll need something to cut dough out of the storage bucket, and either of these works well. Shears are also handy for cutting pita bread, or even pizza, and you'll need a pair to cut the *pain d'épi* before baking (page 92).

Stand mixer, food processor: For an easier alternative to mixing dough by hand, you can use a 5- or 6-quart heavy-duty stand mixer (with the paddle/flat beater) or a 14-cup food processor (with a dough attachment). Your mixer or

---

food processor must be large enough to handle a full batch of our dough, which weighs about 4 pounds and uses about 7 cups of flour. If you don't know the capacity of your machine, check with the manufacturer. Some food processors don't make a perfect seal at the bottom, so you may need to add the dry ingredients first and then pour in the liquids; otherwise it will leak. Stop the machine as soon as the ingredients are uniformly mixed.

Immersion blender: This tool is great for breaking up a lump of old dough, known in French as *pâte fermentée* (pot fair-mon-táy). Pâte fermentée can be used to jump-start the sourdough process for stored dough (see sidebar, page 74). These blenders are also nice for breaking up pieces of whole tomatoes for pizza sauce. Be sure that the immersion blender is fully submerged in any liquid mixture before turning it on; otherwise you'll be spattered with ingredients. **Safety note:** Remember that immersion blenders don't have a protective safety interlock so it's possible to touch the sharp spinning blades while the unit is on.

Pastry brushes: These are used to paint cornstarch wash, egg wash, oil, or water onto the surface of the loaf just before baking, sometimes to provide shine or color, and sometimes to act as a "glue" for seeds or other toppings. Silicone and natural-bristle versions are available—the silicone ones are dishwasher safe while the natural-bristle brushes have to be hand washed, and aren't as durable.

Microplane zester: This rasp-style grater is used for removing the zest from citrus fruit without any of the bitter pith. We use one when we want an assertive citrus flavor that you can't get from the fruit's juice.

Convection ovens: This type of oven speeds baking by circulating hot air around the bread and produces a first-rate brown and crispy crust. Some older convection models specify that temperatures should be lowered 25 degrees to prevent overbrowning, while many recent models make the correction automatically, so check your manual. In some, you'll need to turn the loaf around at the halfway point so that each side will brown evenly. Ignore convection-oven instructions that claim you can skip the preheat—the preheat is necessary for our method, especially if you're using a baking stone. As always, use an oven thermometer to check temperature; air circulation in convection ovens can "fool" thermostats in some models, sometimes driving the temperature up by as much as 75 degrees.

These instructions apply only to range-based convection ovens, not microwaves with convection modes, which we have not tested. But we can say with absolute certainty that ordinary microwave ovens simply do not work for bread-baking. Trust us on this one.

4

TIPS AND TECHNIQUES

This chapter will help you perfect your stored-dough, high-moisture breads. In the discussion that follows, we provide tips and techniques to create breads with a professional-quality crust (exterior) and crumb (interior).

Measuring Ingredients by Weight Rather than Cup Measures

Many readers of our very first book, especially those outside the United States, asked for weight equivalents. In the fourteen years since we wrote that book, American home bakers have gradually come around to weighing flours and other ingredients, rather than using cup measures, because it's easier, quicker, and more consistent. All of our books since 2011 have included weight measures as well as cups.

Using digital scales: Inexpensive digital scales are a snap to use. Simply press the "tare" (zeroing) button after placing your empty mixing vessel on the scale. Then "tare" again before adding each subsequent ingredient. There's less cleanup, and your measurements won't be affected by different scooping styles or how tightly or loosely compacted your flour was in its bin (see page 37).

Measuring small-quantity ingredients: Our recipes only require a fraction of an ounce of salt and yeast. Since most scales for home use are accurate only to the nearest ⅛ ounce (3 or 4 grams), measuring small amounts this way can

introduce inaccuracy—this becomes less important when measuring larger quantities for doubled recipes. Unless you're confident of your scale's accuracy for very small amounts, or you're making a double batch or larger, measure salt and yeast with measuring spoons.

Using a digital scale to improvise: Once you're fluent with our method, you can use a concept called "baker's percentage" for improvisation and experimentation. Start with 1,000 grams of flour to make about 4 to 4½ pounds (1.8 to 2.0 kilograms) of dough. This will be much simpler and more intuitive if you use metric weights (grams and kilograms) rather than U.S. measures (ounces and pounds). Zero out the scale ("tare"), and the fun begins. For our standard recipe for white-flour stored dough on page 63, you can see that the ratio of liquid to flour is 0.75 (75 percent)—that's the baker's percentage of water in this recipe. No, it doesn't mean that the recipe is 75 percent water; again, it only means that the ratio of the weight of water to the weight of flour is 0.75 (75 percent). When we talk about liquids in a recipe, the baker's percentage is called the "hydration" level. Once you understand what our wet dough should look like, you can play with the baker's percentage of liquid (hydration) that's needed to produce a dough that's made partly with whole grains, seeds, or other ingredients. Any ingredient in any of the recipes can be represented as their baker's percentage—professional reference books always work this way, because this method makes it easier to scale up a recipe to any multiple of the original yield. Whole grain flour, rye flour, and high protein flour all need more water than typical all-purpose white flours, so take this into account if you're substituting one for the other. When calculating the flour weight, be sure to total up the weight of all flour types in the recipe. Have fun!

Storing Dough to Develop Flavor

All of our recipes are based on dough that can be stored for up to fourteen days in the refrigerator, depending on ingredients. That makes our method incredibly convenient. But there's another benefit to storing the dough: Sourdough flavor develops over the lifespan of the batch. That means that your first loaves won't taste the same as your last ones. Some of our readers have taken to mixing staggered batches, so that they're never baking with brand-new dough.

How much to make and store: In order to have fresh-baked artisan bread with only five minutes a day of active preparation time, make enough dough to last a week or more. Your initial time investment (mixing the dough) is the most significant one, though it generally takes no more than fifteen minutes. By mixing larger batches, you can spread that investment over more days of bread making. So we recommend mixing enough dough to last at least seven to fourteen days (less for egg-based and some whole grain doughs). For larger households, that might mean doubling or even tripling the recipes. Don't forget to choose a container large enough to accommodate the rising of the larger batch.

Dough Consistency: How Wet Is Wet Enough?

Our recipes were carefully tested, and we arrived at the ratio of wet to dry ingredients with an eye toward creating a relatively slack and wet dough. But flours can vary in their protein content, the degree to which they're compacted into their containers, and in the amount of water they've absorbed from the environment. And environment changes; in most places, humidity will fluctuate over the course of the year. All of this means that our recipes may produce slightly variable results depending on humidity, compaction, and the flour brand you're using.

If you find that your doughs are too stiff, especially if after storage they don't show good "oven spring" (the sudden rising seen soon after going into a hot oven), decrease the flour by ⅛ cup at a time in subsequent batches (or increase the water by a tablespoon). If they're too loose and wet, and don't hold a shape well for free-form loaves, increase the flour, again by ⅛ cup at a time. If you don't want to wait until your next batch to correct a problem with moisture content, you can work extra flour into a too-wet batch (give it some time to absorb after doing this). For too-dry batches, it can be challenging to mix water into the dough—but it can be done. If all else fails, overly wet dough still works well as flatbread, or in loaf pans. The same is true for dough nearing the end of its storage life.

You can vary the moisture level in our recipes based on your taste. Here's what you can expect:

If you modify a recipe, using . . .	
more liquid or less flour (giving you wetter dough), you'll get . . .	**less liquid or more flour (giving you drier dough), you'll get . . .**
Larger air holes	Smaller air holes
Desirable "custard" crumb (below); can become gummy if too little flour is used	Drier crumb (interior); desirable custard crumb will be difficult to achieve
Free-form loaves that may have difficulty holding a shape and spread sideways, but do well in loaf pans or as flatbread.	Free-form loaves that hold their shape well and remain high and domed
Dough that requires less resting time before baking	Dough that requires more resting time before baking

"Custard" Crumb

Perfectly baked high-moisture dough can produce a delightful "custard" crumb (interior). When mixed with water and baked, wheat flour's protein, mostly gluten, traps the water and creates a chewy and moist texture, with air holes that have shiny walls. As you adjust flour amounts for your favorite recipes, you'll find that this is an effect you can manipulate. Too much flour, and you will lose the "custard" crumb character. Too little, and the dough will be difficult to shape and the crumb may be gummy.

Resting and Baking Times Are Approximate

All of our resting and baking times are approximate. Since loaves are formed by hand, their size will vary from loaf to loaf, which means their resting and baking time requirements will vary as well. In general, flat or skinny loaves don't need much resting time and will bake rapidly. High-domed loaves will require longer resting and baking times. So unless you're weighing out exact 1-pound loaves and forming the same shapes each time, your resting and baking times will vary, and our listed times should be seen only as a starting point.

In our very first book, in 2007, we recommended a resting time of forty minutes for 1-pound, round loaves made from lean dough (see page 55). We were very sensitive to the beginning baker's time constraints—if it took too long, even for passive resting times, people might not bake the bread. And most of our readers were happy with the result they got with the forty-minute rest. But others said they'd be willing to try a longer rest to get an airier crumb. For those folks, we started recommending a range of rest times for a  1-pounder: forty to ninety minutes, especially if your kitchen is cool. The longer rest will give you a more open hole structure and a loftier result. This is more important when you are using whole grains in the loaf. If you extend the resting time beyond forty minutes, or if your environment is particularly dry, cover the loaf with plastic wrap or a roomy overturned bowl—this prevents the surface from drying out and forming a crust that might inhibit rising and oven spring. Skinny loaves (like baguettes, page 88) or flatbreads (Chapter 9) do well with the shorter resting times; in fact, pizza and many flatbreads need none at all. Here are some guidelines for varying resting and baking times:

Increase resting and/or baking time if any of the following apply:

- The temperature of your kitchen is low: This only affects rising and resting times, not baking.
- You're baking a larger loaf: A 2-pound, free-form, white loaf takes a ninety-minute resting time and forty-five to fifty minutes to bake. A tall, domed, 3-pound loaf will require a two-hour resting time and nearly an hour to bake (not so much if the loaf is flattish).
- You're using more whole grain than we call for in a recipe.

Baking Temperature Is Based on Dough Ingredients:

- Most non-enriched doughs: 450°F
- Most egg, honey, or brioche doughs: 350°F

A good rule of thumb for resting time after shaping: If you want loaves to develop maximum rise and air holes, wait until the dough no longer feels dense and cold. A well-rested loaf will begin to feel "jiggly" when you shake it on its peel—like set Jell-O.

Preparing the Pizza Peel—Grains or Parchment Paper?

Many of our recipes call for sliding the loaf off a pizza peel directly onto a hot baking stone. Cornmeal is a traditional "lubricant," but it's only one of many options. We tend to use cornmeal on the peel for the more rustic, full-flavored loaves and whole wheat flour for the more delicate breads, like the French baguette. White flour serves the same purpose under pita and *ciabatta*. Coarser grains like cornmeal are the most slippery, and fine-ground flours may require a heavier coating to prevent sticking (sometimes you'll have to nudge the loaves off with a spatula or dough scraper). Mostly though, the choice of grain on the pizza peel is a matter of taste. We've used Malt-O-Meal cereal or oatmeal in a pinch, and Zoë's mom once used grits. If you're having trouble sliding loaves off a pizza peel prepared with grain, or if you want to keep your oven neat and clean, switch to parchment paper (see page 34).

Underbaking Problems

The crust is crispy when it emerges from the oven, but it softens as it comes to room temperature: The bread may be underbaked. This is most often a problem with large breads, but it can happen with any loaf. Internal moisture, so high in wet dough, doesn't dissipate in underbaked bread, so it redistributes to the crust as the bread cools. As you gain experience, you'll be able to judge just how brown the loaf must be to prevent this problem with any given loaf size. We use brownness and crust firmness as our measure of doneness (there will be a few blackened bits on the loaf in non-egg breads). You can also insert a thin-bladed knife into the center of the loaf, which should come out clean (cake-testers aren't good for this purpose). And while we're not confident of the accuracy of instant-read thermometers that are inserted into food to check temperature, they're a good substitute for the knife to be sure the interior isn't wet.

The loaf has a soggy or gummy crumb:

- Check your oven temperature with a thermometer.
- Be sure that you're adequately preheating your stone and oven, and consider a longer preheat (see page 54).

- Make sure you are allowing the dough to rest for the full time period we've recommended.
- Be sure you're measuring your flour and liquids correctly, whether you opt for measuring cups or a scale.
- Your dough may benefit from being a little drier. For the next batch, increase the flour by ⅛ cup (or decrease the liquids a little) and check the result.
- If you're baking a large loaf (more than 1 pound), rest and bake it longer (see page 47).

Top crust won't crisp and brown:

- Use a baking stone when called for, and preheat it for at least twenty minutes in an oven whose temperature has been checked with a thermometer.
- Bake with steam when called for. Use one of the methods described on page 28.
- Try the shelf switcheroo. If you're a crisp-crust fanatic, here's the ultimate approach for baking the perfect crust: Place the stone on the bottom rack and start the loaf there. Two-thirds of the way through baking, transfer the loaf from the stone directly to the top rack of the oven (leave the stone where it is). Top crusts brown best near the top of the oven, and bottom crusts brown best near the bottom. This approach works beautifully with free-form loaves, but also helps crisp the crust of hard-crusted loaf-pan breads: Just pop the bread out of the pan before transferring to the top rack—it makes a big difference. With this approach, you can permanently park your baking stone on the very lowest rack, where it will help even out the heat for everything you bake, not just bread. Then there'll be no need to shift around the stone or racks to accommodate your bread-baking habit.
- Bake with convection, which can improve crust color.

Overbaking Problems, Dry Patches

The crust is great, but the crumb (interior) is dry:

- The bread may be overbaked. Make sure your oven is calibrated properly using an oven thermometer, and double-check your baking time.
- The dough may have been dry to begin with. In traditional recipes, there's usually an instruction that reads something like "knead thoroughly, until the mass of dough is smooth, elastic, and less sticky, adding flour as needed." This often means too much flour gets added. Be careful not to work in additional flour when shaping.

There are flour blobs in the middle of the loaf: Be sure to completely mix the initial batch. Using wet hands to incorporate the last bits of flour will often take

Don't slice or eat loaves when they're still warm, unless they're flatbreads, rolls, or very skinny baguettes. The proteins continue to cook and set as the bread cools. Warm bread has a certain romance, so we know that it's hard to wait for it to cool. But waiting will improve the texture—loaf breads are at their peak of flavor and texture about two hours after they come out of the oven (or whenever they completely cool). Hot or warm bread cuts poorly (the slices collapse and seem gummy) and dries out quickly, and these problems are exaggerated with high-moisture dough. Use a sharp serrated bread knife to go right through the crisp crust and soft crumb. Flatbreads, rolls, and skinny baguettes are different—their size makes them easier to bake through despite the high-moisture dough, so you can enjoy them warm.

care of this. The culprit is sometimes the shaping step—extra flour can get tucked up under and inside the loaf as it's formed. Use lots of dusting flour, but allow most of it to fall off.

Issues Specific to Gluten-Free Baking

If your gluten-free bread is dense, doughy, or heavy, with poor hole structure:

- **If you're hand mixing, consider switching to a stand mixer or food processor** (see page 37). Some people have trouble getting a smooth gluten-free mixture when they mix by hand. If your hand-mixed dough is lumpy, this can give you a dense loaf. If you're not happy with a hand-mixed batch, you can put it in a stand mixer, fitted with a paddle attachment, and let it run on high for thirty seconds to a minute. Let the dough rest for at least an hour before using as directed in the recipe.
- **Make sure that your dough is not too wet or too dry:** Both extremes will result in a dense crumb. If you're measuring gluten-free flour by volume, make sure you are measuring by packing flour into the cup. And if you're getting inconsistent results, consider weighing the flour with a digital scale rather than measuring it out with measuring cups (see page 41).

Frequently Asked Questions (FAQs) from Readers

"WHY DON'T THE LOAVES RISE MUCH DURING THE RESTING PERIOD AFTER SHAPING?"

Compared with traditional doughs, our breads get more of their total rise from "oven spring" (sudden expansion of gases inside the loaf that occurs on contact with hot oven air and baking stone)—and less from "proofing" (the resting time after a loaf is shaped, before baking). So don't be surprised if you don't see much rising during our resting step. You'll still get a nice rise from oven spring, so long as you didn't overwork the dough while shaping. If you want to coax a little more rise during the resting period, try prolonging it (see page 45). And make sure your oven's up to temperature by checking with a thermometer (see page 32). If the oven is too cool or too hot, you won't get proper oven spring.

"WHY DO MY LOAVES SPREAD SIDEWAYS RATHER THAN RISING VERTICALLY?"

Since our dough is wet, it can be less structured than traditional dough. Even when their loaves expanded well and had good air bubbles before baking, readers sometimes got free-form loaves that didn't hold their shape and spread sideways during baking rather than rising upward. The bread was delicious, but it didn't make tall sandwich slices. Often, the cause is insufficient "gluten-cloaking" (sidebar, page 70), the stretching of the outside of the dough around itself during the shaping step. Take a look at the video at BreadIn5.com/GlutenCloak, and be sure to use enough dusting flour when you shape loaves. If you continue to find that your loaves spread sideways, you can dry out the dough by increasing the flour (1/8 cup per batch).

And if your dough is nearing or exceeding the end of its storage life, consider using it for pizza or flatbread. Those don't need much structure—they're flat in the first place and don't need to support the weight of a heavy loaf.

"MY LOAVES ARE TOO DENSE AND HEAVY—WHAT AM I DOING WRONG?"

If your bread is dense, doughy, or heavy, with poor hole structure . . .

1. **Make sure that your dough is not too wet or too dry;** both extremes

---

will result in a dense crumb. Some white flours need a little extra water or you'll get a dry dough—see page 12 for adjustments. If you're measuring flour by volume, make sure you are using the **scoop-and-sweep method** that we describe in Chapter 5, and view our video at BreadIn5.com/ScoopAndSweep. And if you're getting inconsistent results, consider weighing the flour rather than measuring it out with measuring cups (see page 41), using a digital scale.

2. **Be quick and gentle when shaping loaves:** We find that many bakers, especially experienced ones, want to knead the dough—but you can't do that with this kind of dough, or you will knock the gas out of it and the result will be a dense crumb. When shaping our doughs, you're trying to preserve gas bubbles as much as possible—these bubbles create the holes in the bread. Shape your loaves in only twenty to forty seconds.

3. **Try a longer rest after shaping, especially if your kitchen is cool or you're making a large loaf** (see page 45).

4. **You may prefer longer-stored dough for pizza or flatbread:** If you are using a dough that is nearing the end of its batch-life, you may want to stick to pizza, pita, naan, or another option from the flatbread chapter (page 157), or from our third book, *Artisan Pizza and Flatbread in Five Minutes a Day* (2011). As the dough ages it produces denser results when you use it for loaves—many of our readers love it a little dense, but others use the older stuff for flatbreads. If you prefer your dough "younger," you can freeze it when it begins to produce denser loaves.

5. **Check your oven temperature:** If your oven's temperature is off, whether too warm or too cool, you won't get proper "oven spring" and the loaf will be dense, with a pale or burnt crust. Use an oven thermometer (see page 32) to ensure that you're baking at the correct temperature.

6. **Try the "refrigerator rise" trick:** By using the refrigerator, you can shape your dough and then have it rise in the refrigerator for eight to fourteen hours. First thing in the morning, cut off a piece of dough and shape it as normal. Place the dough on a sheet of parchment paper, loosely wrap with plastic or cover it with an overturned bowl, and put it back in the refrigerator. Right before dinner, preheat your oven with a stone on a middle rack and take the loaf out of the refrigerator. You may find that it has spread slightly, and may not have risen much, but it will still have lovely oven spring. Because you don't handle the dough at all after the refrigerator rise, the bubbles in the dough should still be intact. A twenty- to thirty-minute rest on the counter while preheating is all you need. Then slash and bake as usual.

"WHAT DO I DO ABOUT CHANGES IN THE DOUGH TOWARD THE END OF ITS STORAGE LIFE? AND WHY DOES MY DOUGH LOOK GRAY?"

Especially if you don't bake every day, you may find that toward the end of a batch's storage life, its entire surface darkens (or even turns gray) and it develops a more intense sourdough flavor; dark liquid may collect. None of this is mold or spoilage—don't toss it, just pour off the liquid, and work in enough flour to absorb excess moisture in the dough. Then rest the dough for two hours at room temperature before using. If you are not using it right away, refrigerate it again; you can keep it until the end of the dough's recommended life.

If a gray leathery coating develops on the surface of the dough, you can usually just turn that to the interior of the loaf as you shape it. It may cause a dense layer in the crumb, so remove it if you prefer.

Discard any dough that develops mold on its surface, which you can identify as dark or light patches, with or without a fuzzy appearance.

"SHOULD I PREHEAT THE STONE FOR LONGER THAN YOU RECOMMEND?"

Professionals sometimes suggest preheating the baking stone for an hour to absorb all the heat it possibly can, but we specify a shorter time in our recipes. Many of our readers expressed concern about wasted energy with a long preheat, not to mention the need for more advance planning. So we compromised—we know that some ovens will produce a crisper crust with a longer preheat, but we're pretty happy with the results we get at twenty to thirty minutes (even though many ovens equipped with a stone won't quite achieve target temperature that soon). If you find that the crust isn't as crisp as you like, or the baking time is longer than expected, try increasing the preheating time to forty-five or even sixty minutes. It's not essential but it can be useful, especially with a thicker stone.

Cast-iron "stones" (see page 30) and ¼-inch-thick ceramic stones heat up faster than ½-inch-thick ceramic ones, so consider those if you're committed to the shortest possible preheat.

"WHY DO I GET ODDLY SHAPED LOAVES?"

If you haven't used enough cornmeal on the pizza peel, a spot of dough may stick to it. As you slide the loaf off the peel, the spot pulls, causing an odd-shaped loaf. Prevent this by using more cornmeal on the pizza peel, especially if the dough is particularly sticky, or switch to parchment paper (see page 34).

If your loaves are cracking along the bottom or bulging on the sides, it is generally due to one or both of these issues:

- Not slashing deeply enough—be sure to slash ½-inch-deep cuts straight down into the dough.

- Not letting the shaped loaves rest long enough before baking. Consider a longer resting time, especially if your environment is cool (see page 45) or your dough feels dry.

And if your loaves seem to "pull up" from the bottom crust as they bake, it's a sign of a dried-out top crust. Consider covering with plastic wrap or a roomy overturned bowl during the resting phase.

"WHAT ARE 'LEAN' AND 'ENRICHED' DOUGHS?"

Lean doughs are those made without significant amounts of eggs, fat, dairy, or sweetener. They bake well without burning or drying out at high temperatures. Doughs enriched with lots of eggs, fat, dairy, or sweeteners require a lower baking temperature (and a longer baking time), because eggs and sweetener can burn at high temperatures (the oil isn't the problem).

"WHAT'S THE BEST WAY TO STORE FRESH BREAD?"

The best way to preserve a crisp lean-dough loaf after it's been cut is to place it cut-side down on a flat, nonporous surface like a plate or a clean countertop. If you store it in foil or plastic, it'll last longer without drying out, but trapped moisture will soften the crust. Pita bread's different—it's supposed to have a soft crust and stores nicely in a plastic bag or airtight container once cooled. Breads made with whole grain flour and those made with dough that has been well aged stay fresh longest. You can also freeze baked loaves in zipped plastic bags (or doubled supermarket produce bags), and consider pre-slicing them (see sidebar, page 87).

"I can't resist fresh bread!" Bread is my weakness, too, so I feel your pain. I've always struggled to stay disciplined when testing recipes, and now that my wife, Laura, and I are empty nesters, we can't count on our kids to help us polish off a fresh boule, peasant loaf, or French bread. I have the hardest time with free-form loaves that you can hack away at all day long, easily eating half a loaf a day. So now I keep bread on hand in one of three ways: I only bake the portion-size we plan to eat (e.g., a half-pound boule or two 3-ounce pitas); I freeze 8-ounce portions of dough and thaw them out the night before I plan to bake them; or I make 2-pound loaf-pan breads, then slice and freeze them (see page 85) in zipped plastic bags or doubled supermarket produce bags. If slices stick together they can be chiseled apart with a table knife before defrosting or toasting. Whole grain or rye loaves freeze especially well.—Jeff

"CAN I FREEZE THE DOUGH?"

Our dough can be frozen at any point in its batch-life, so long as the initial rise has been completed. It's best to divide it into loaf-sized, well-dusted portions and then wrap it very well or seal it in airtight containers, zipped plastic bags, or doubled supermarket produce bags, which have the added benefit of being free. Defrost overnight in the fridge when ready to use and then shape, rest, and bake as usual. How long to freeze is partly a matter of taste—our dough loses some rising power when frozen and some people find the results dense if it's frozen for too long. That's especially true for enriched doughs, such as challah and brioche. Here are some basic guidelines for maximum freezing times for dough:

- Lean dough (no eggs and minimal butter or oil): four weeks
- Challah (page 187): three weeks

- Brioche (page 195): two weeks
- Gluten-free dough (pages 173–82): two weeks

"WHY DOES MY DOUGH HAVE A YEAST OR ALCOHOL SMELL?

Some people detect a yeasty or alcohol aroma or flavor in the dough, and that's no surprise—yeast multiplies in dough, creating alcohol and carbon dioxide gas as it ferments sugars and starches. The alcohol will boil off during baking, but our stored dough develops character from the by-products of yeast fermentation; most people appreciate the flavor and aroma of this mild sourdough. But others want less of that, so here are some things to try:

- Always vent the rising container as directed, especially in the first two days of storage (see pages 32–33). You can even poke a tiny hole in the lid to allow gas to escape.
- Consider a low-yeast version of our recipes (see page 19).
- Store your dough for shorter periods than we specify, freezing the remainder. Or make smaller batches so they're used up more quickly.

"CAN I ADD NATURAL SOURDOUGH STARTER TO THE RECIPES?"

Yes, sourdough starter works in our recipes, and there's much more on this in Chapter 12.

"HOW DO I BAKE AT HIGH ALTITUDE?"

There can be a big difference in how yeast behaves if you live much above 5,280 feet (1,610 meters). With less air pressure constraining the rising dough, it balloons up too quickly, and then collapses abruptly, giving you a dense result. The following adjustments can help you avoid that by slowing down the initial rise (the dough won't be ready for the refrigerator in the usual two hours):

- Decrease the yeast by half or even more (see page 19).
- Use bread flour to increase the strength of the dough, but you will also have to increase the water (see page 12).
- Assuming you like the flavor and aren't on a salt-restricted diet, consider a saltier dough—salt inhibits fast yeast growth. If you go this route, use the higher end of our salt range in the ingredient lists.
- Decrease sugar if there's any in the recipe—it feeds yeast.
- Do the initial dough rise overnight in the refrigerator (see the refrigerator-rise trick, page 53), and consider mixing the dough using cold liquids.

These techniques allow the dough to rise more slowly, giving it more time to achieve full height without collapsing.

"HOW DO I KEEP BAKING ON THE GAS GRILL IN THE SUMMER?"

For those hot summer days when you want fresh bread but can't stand the idea of turning on the oven, outdoor covered gas grills are one answer (or try crock pot baking on page 105). When baking on a grill, thinner is better. Flatbreads and pizza are the easiest (see Chapter 9), but if you keep them skinny (like baguettes), loaf breads work, too. Stick with lean doughs—they're more resistant to scorching.

1. **Form a free-form loaf (make it skinny and long) or an oblong-shaped flatbread with your favorite recipe.** Pay attention to the shape so it will fit between the gas grill burners and bake over *indirect* heat (the flames

aren't right underneath the bread). Allow to rest on a pizza peel; parchment paper can be helpful in preventing scorching, but it isn't required. If you keep it really thin, as an elongated flatbread narrow enough to fit mostly between the burner flames (⅛ to ¼ inch thick), you don't need any resting time.

2. **Preheat the grill** with burners set to high, but decrease to low just before placing the loaf right on the grate—between the gas grill burners so it isn't exposed to direct grill flames. Slash if you're doing a loaf bread. **Close the grill cover to retain heat.** You may need to experiment with the heat setting—grill brands differ, and it may help to shut off one of the burners.

3. Open the grill in four to fifteen minutes (depending on loaf thickness), **turn the loaf over,** and finish on the second side for another four to fifteen minutes. You may need to briefly expose the loaf to direct heat in order to achieve browning.

If your grilled breads are burning, experiment with a baking stone, which shields the loaf from scorching grill heat (cast-iron "stones" or baking steels will be more crack-resistant on the grill). If you opt for a stone, you can achieve nice crust-browning with a moisture-trapping metal bowl or aluminum foil roasting pan covering the loaf, but you'll probably still need to turn the loaf at the midpoint to get top-browning. Remove the bowl or pan for the last third of the baking time. You can also use a covered cast-iron pot or a cloche (see page 29) on the grill (preheat the top and bottom before putting in the loaf). If these scorch the bottom crust, line the pot or cloche with crumpled aluminum foil and use parchment paper between the loaf and the foil. Or put a baking stone on the grill underneath the pot, to shield it from scorching heat. Bake two-thirds of the baking time closed, then uncover for the last third (but keep the grill cover closed).

"HOW DO I PARBAKE ARTISAN LOAVES?"

Parbaking means partially baking your loaves and finishing the baking later. Parbaked bread can even be frozen. The perfect opportunity for this approach? You are invited to your friends' home for dinner. Parbake the loaf at home and complete the baking in their oven—you'll be able to present absolutely fresh bread or rolls for the dinner party.

Baking instructions for parbaked bread:

1. Follow preparation steps for any recipe in this book.

2. Begin baking at the recipe's usual temperature.

3. Remove the loaf from the oven when it just begins to darken in color; the idea is to just set the center of the loaf. For most loaves, that means nearly 90 percent of the baking time.

4. Allow the loaf to cool on a rack and then place in a plastic bag. Freeze immediately if you plan to wait more than half a day to finish baking.

To complete the baking:

1. If frozen, completely defrost the loaf, still wrapped, at room temperature. Unwrap the defrosted loaf, place it on a preheated baking stone or directly on the oven rack, and bake at the recipe's recommended temperature. Bake until browned and appealing, usually five to ten minutes.

2. Allow to cool on a rack as usual.

Conversion Tables for Common Liquid Measures

Volumes

U.S. Spoon- and Cup-Measures	U.S. Liquid Volume	Metric Volume
1 teaspoon	$\frac{1}{6}$ ounce	5 ml
1 tablespoon	$\frac{1}{2}$ ounce	15 ml
$\frac{1}{4}$ cup	2 ounces	60 ml
$\frac{1}{2}$ cup	4 ounces	120 ml
1 cup	8 ounces	240 ml
2 cups	16 ounces	475 ml
4 cups	32 ounces	950 ml

Oven Temperature: Fahrenheit to Celsius Conversion

Degrees Fahrenheit	Degrees Celsius
350	180
375	190
400	200
425	220
450	230
475	240
500	250
550	288

Visit BreadIn5.com, where you'll find recipes, photos, videos, and instructional material.

5

THE MASTER RECIPE

We chose an artisan free-form loaf that the French call a boule—
pronounced "bool," meaning "ball"—as the basic model for all the breads
in this book (see cover photo). You'll learn a truly revolutionary approach to
bread baking with this master recipe: Take the needed amount of pre-mixed
dough from the refrigerator, shape it, leave it to rest, then pop it in the oven and
let it bake while you're preparing the rest of the meal.

This dough is made with nothing but all-purpose flour, yeast, salt, and water,

and it's the easiest to handle, shape, and bake. It's incredibly versatile and can be used to create a wide variety of shapes and styles. You'll learn how wet the dough needs to be (wet, but not so wet that the finished loaf won't hold its shape) and how a "gluten cloak" substitutes for kneading. Wetter doughs encourage the development of sourdough character over two weeks of storage. And by omitting kneading, by mixing dough in bulk, and by storing and using it as it's needed over time, you'll truly be able to make this bread in five minutes a day (excluding resting and oven time).

You should become familiar with the following recipe before going through the rest of the book.

The Master Recipe: Boule (Artisan Free-Form Loaf)

Makes four loaves, slightly less than 1 pound each. The recipe can be doubled or halved.

Ingredient	Volume (U.S.)	Weight (U.S.)	Weight (Metric)
Lukewarm water (100°F or below)	3 cups	1 pound, 8 ounces	680 grams
Granulated yeast[1]	1 tablespoon	0.35 ounce	10 grams
Kosher salt[1]	1 to 1½ tablespoons	0.6 to 0.9 ounce	17 to 25 grams
All-purpose flour	6½ cups (scoop-and-sweep)	2 pounds	910 grams
Cornmeal or parchment paper, for the pizza peel			

[1]Can adjust to taste (see pages 18 and 20).

Mixing and Storing the Dough

1. **Warm the water slightly:** It should feel just a little warmer than body temperature, about 100°F. When made with warm water, the dough will rise to the right point for storage in about 2 hours. You can use cold water and get the same final result, but the first rising will take longer (see page 17).

2. **Add yeast and salt to the water** in a 6-quart bowl or, preferably, in a lidded (not airtight) food container, food-grade plastic bucket, or a non-reactive soup pot. Don't worry about getting it all to dissolve.

Does salted water harm the yeast? Some traditional recipes mention the risk of suppressing yeast activity if you allow yeast to come directly into contact with salted water, so they often recommend whisking salt into the flour rather than putting the salt into the water. We've found that with a full tablespoon of modern granulated yeast, this just doesn't matter. If you're worried about this, or if you're not getting the rise you want (or you're not getting it fast enough), especially with low-yeast variations (page 19), whisk the salt into the dry flour before adding dry ingredients to yeasted water.

"My yeast is clumping in the water!" It's not a big deal if the yeast doesn't completely dissolve, but if you gently sprinkle the yeast evenly all over the surface of the water, and let it sit, undisturbed, for three to five minutes, the granules hydrate separately and won't clump. Then mix as usual.

3. **Mix in the flour—kneading is unnecessary:** Add all of the flour at once, measuring it first with dry-ingredient measuring cups, or by weighing the ingredients (preferred). If you measure with cups, use the scoop-and-sweep method, gently scooping up flour with a sideways motion, then sweeping the top level with a knife or spatula; don't press down

The scoop-and-sweep method: It's easier to scoop and sweep if you store your flour in a bin rather than the bag it's sold in; it can be difficult to get the measuring cups into the bag without making a mess. Don't use an extra-large, 2-cup-capacity measuring cup, which allows the flour to overpack and measures too much flour. And consider weighing flour—it's more accurate (see Tips and Techniques, page 41).

into the flour as you scoop or you'll throw off the measurement by compressing (see our video on this at BreadIn5.com/ScoopAndSweep).

Mix with a wooden spoon, Danish dough whisk, or a heavy-duty stand mixer until the mixture is uniform. For most stand mixers, the paddle attachment works best with our high-moisture dough (some manufacturers call this the "flat beater"). In large-capacity mixers (6-quart or larger), the dough hook works better. If you're hand-mixing and it becomes too difficult to incorporate all the flour with the spoon, you can reach into your mixing vessel with very wet hands and press the mixture together. Don't knead! It isn't necessary. You're finished when everything is uniformly moist, without dry patches. This step is done in a matter of minutes and will yield a dough that is wet and loose enough to conform to the shape of its container.

Other tools to use for the initial mixing: If you're mixing by hand, a **Danish dough whisk** (page 36) is a nice alternative to a wooden spoon. It's much stouter than a flimsy egg-beating whisk, and it incorporates the wet and dry ingredients in no time flat. **Food processors** also work well—just replace the standard blade with the dough attachment that comes with most machines. Make sure the machine is rated to handle dough—the motor must be heavy duty. You'll also need the largest size made to mix a full batch—one with a 14-cup bowl. Make a half batch if your processor has a smaller bowl and stop the machine as soon as the ingredients are uniformly mixed (see page 37).

4. **Allow to rise:** Cover with a lid that fits the container but can be cracked open so it's not completely airtight—most plastic lids fit the bill. If you're using a bowl, cover it loosely with plastic wrap. If you're using a soup pot, the lid won't be airtight so that's a good option as well. Towels don't work—they stick to wet dough. Lidded (or even vented) plastic buckets are readily available (see page 32). Allow the mixture to rise at room temperature until it begins to collapse (or at least slightly flattens on the top), about 2 hours, depending on the room's temperature and the initial water temperature—then refrigerate it and use over the next 14 days. If your container isn't vented, leave it open a crack for the first couple of days in the fridge to allow gases to escape— after that you can usually close it. If you forget about your rising dough on the counter, don't worry: longer rising times at room temperature, even overnight, will not harm the result (though egg-enriched dough should go into the fridge after 2 hours). You can use a portion of the dough any time after the 2-hour rise. Fully refrigerated wet dough is less sticky and easier to work with than room-temperature dough, so the first time you try our method, it's best to refrigerate the dough over-night (or for at least 3 hours) before shaping a loaf. Once refrigerated, the dough will seem to have shrunk back upon itself, and it will never rise again in the bucket—that's normal. **Do not punch down this dough.** With our method, the dough needs to retain as much gas as possible; punching it down will knock out the gas and make your loaves denser.

On Baking Day

5. **The gluten cloak: Don't knead. Just "cloak" and shape a loaf in 20 to 40 seconds** (see sidebar, page 70). Prepare a pizza peel with cornmeal or

parchment paper, which will prevent your loaf from sticking to it when you slide it into the oven (the parchment paper slides right onto the stone along with the loaf). Dust the surface of your refrigerated dough with flour. Pull up and cut off a 1-pound (grapefruit-size) piece of dough, using a serrated knife or kitchen shears. Hold the dough and add more flour as needed so it won't stick to your hands. Gently stretch the surface of the dough around to the bottom on all 4 sides, rotating the ball a quarter-turn as you go. Most of the dusting flour will fall off; it's not intended to be incorporated into the dough. The bottom of the loaf may appear to be a collection of bunched ends, but it will flatten out and adhere during resting and baking. A properly shaped loaf will be smooth and cohesive, but don't worry about it on your first try—this

What's a gluten cloak? Just imagine a warm blanket being pulled around you on a cold night. Or, for the more technically inclined: Gluten-cloaking aligns the protein strands in the surface of the dough. By adding just enough flour to create a resilient "cloak" around the mass of wet dough, you help the dough to hold its shape during the expansion that will happen during baking. As you shape, it's as if you're pulling a cloak around the dough, so that the entire ball is surrounded by a taut skin. *Resist the temptation* to get rid of all stickiness by incorporating too much flour. This could prevent the bread from developing a finished crumb with the appealing artisanal "custard" (see page 44) and leave you with a dry loaf. See our video on gluten-cloaking at BreadIn5.com/GlutenCloak.

Adjusting the resting time:

- **Lengthen the resting time** if your fridge or the room is particularly cold, if you're making larger loaves, or if you just want to get a more open and airy crumb structure. You can go as long as 90 minutes for a 1-pound loaf. When increasing the resting time, especially in dry environments, cover the loaf with plastic wrap or a roomy overturned bowl—plastic wrap won't stick if the surface is well dusted. Don't use a damp towel—that will stick. And err on the side of longer resting times when baking whole grain bread.

- **You can shorten the resting time by half** if you're using fresh, unrefrigerated dough.

recipe is very forgiving and your next attempts will be better. The entire process should take no more than 20 to 40 seconds—don't work the dough longer or your loaves may be too dense.

6. **Rest the loaf and let it rise on a pizza peel:** Place the shaped ball on the prepared pizza peel, and allow it to rest for about 40 minutes. It doesn't need to be covered during the rest period unless you're extending the rest time to get a more "open" crumb (see sidebar, page 70, and Tips and Techniques, page 45). You may not see much rise during this period; much more rising will occur during baking ("oven spring").

7. **Preheat a baking stone near the middle of the oven to 450°F,** which takes about 20 to 30 minutes. (You can consider a longer preheat; see page 54). Place an empty metal broiler tray for holding water on any rack that won't interfere with the rising bread. **Never use a glass pan to catch water for steam—it's likely to shatter.**

8. **Dust and slash:** Dust the top of the loaf liberally with flour, which will prevent the knife from sticking. Slash a ½-inch-deep cross, scallop, or tic-tac-toe pattern into the top, using a serrated bread knife held perpendicular to the bread—slashing allows the loaf to expand more

Don't have a pizza peel and baking stone? You can rest the formed loaf on a heavy-duty baking sheet prepared with oil, butter, parchment paper, or a silicone mat rated to 450°F. Place the loaf and baking sheet on an oven rack when ready to bake.

evenly and prevents unpredictable and unattractive cracking when the loaf goes through "oven spring" upon hitting the hot stone and oven air (see photos). Leave the flour in place for baking (tap some of it off before eating).

9. **Baking with steam—slide the loaf onto the preheated stone:** Place the tip of the peel a few inches beyond where you want the bread to land. Give the peel a few quick forward-and-back jiggles, and pull it sharply out from under the loaf. Quickly but carefully pour about 1 cup of hot water from the tap into the broiler tray and close the oven door to trap the steam (see page 28 for steam alternatives). Avoid getting water on non-tempered glass oven windows to prevent cracking, or consider covering the window with a towel, removing it before closing the oven door. **If you used parchment paper instead of cornmeal, pull it out from under the loaf after about 20 minutes** for a crisper bottom crust. Bake for a total of 30 to 35 minutes, or until the crust is richly browned and firm to the touch.

Because the dough is wet, there is little risk of drying out the interior, despite the dark crust. (Smaller or larger loaves will require adjustments in baking time; see page 46). When you remove the loaf from the oven, a perfectly baked loaf will

〜

Instant-read thermometers: We're not in love with internal-temperature food ther-mometers, usually sold as "instant-read" thermometers (as opposed to oven thermom-eters, which we love; see page 32). They have a pointed probe that you stick into the bread to see if it's reached a target temperature. We find that the inexpensive ones (under twenty dollars) aren't all that "instant," which means that you're never sure how long to wait before the read-out stabilizes (though they're good for checking for under-baked dough in the center of your loaf). The truly instant (and accurate) digital units are much more expensive (but can still give misleading results if the probe isn't well cen-tered in the loaf). If you have confidence in your thermometer and your technique, here are some guidelines for fully baked bread:

- Lean dough (no eggs): 205°F to 210°F (96°C to 99°C)

- Egg-enriched dough, such as challah and brioche: 180°F to 185°F (82°C to 85°C)

audibly crackle, or "sing," when initially exposed to room-temperature air—and of course, it will be beautiful (see cover photo). Allow to cool completely (up to 2 hours), preferably on a wire cooling rack, for best flavor, texture, and slicing. The crust may initially soften, but will firm up again when cooled. If you're not getting the browning and crispness you want, test your oven temperature with an inexpensive oven ther-mometer (see page 32).

10. **Store the remaining dough in the refrigerator in your lidded or loosely plastic-wrapped container and use it over the next 14 days:** You'll find that even 1 day's storage improves the flavor and texture of your bread.

This maturation continues over the 14-day storage period. If you store your dough in your mixing container, you'll avoid some cleanup. Cut off and shape more loaves as you need them. We often have several types of dough stored in our refrigerators at once. Lean doughs like this (those made without eggs, sweetener, or fat) can be frozen in 1-pound portions in an airtight container for up to 4 weeks and defrosted overnight in the refrigerator before use.

FLAVOR BOOSTERS!

1. **Use a lazy sourdough shortcut:** When your dough bucket is finally empty, or nearly so, don't wash it. Immediately remix another batch in the same container. In addition to saving the cleanup step, leaving the aged dough stuck to the sides of the container will give your new batch a head start on sourdough flavor. Just scrape it down and it will hydrate and incorporate into the new dough. Don't do this with egg- or dairy-enriched dough—with those, the container should be washed after each use. You can take this even further by adding a more sizable amount of old dough from your last batch. You can use up to 2 cups; just mix it in with the water for your new batch and let it stand until it becomes soupy before you start mixing. An immersion blender is helpful for blending the old dough with water, but not required. Add to the dry ingredients in your chosen recipe, as usual. Professionals call this pâte fermentée (pot fair-mon-táy), which means nothing more than "fermented dough." See safety note on immersion blenders (page 38).

2. **Use just a little rye flour:** Rye flour adds tremendous flavor to a white loaf. Adding just one tablespoon to the white-flour Master Recipe makes a noticeable difference, especially as the dough ages. Whole wheat flour is a good second choice.

3. **Use the higher level of salt:** Salt accentuates the flavor of wheat, which is a subtle flavor to begin with. We give a range of salt (1 to 1½ tablespoons) to accommodate differences in taste and to account for health concerns. If you're not on a salt-restricted diet and you're finding the loaves bland (especially early in the batch-life), consider using the higher end of the salt range. As always, be careful with salt of varying coarseness, and measure accordingly (see page 20). This can really become noticeable at the higher end of our salt range.

4. **Stagger your batches and only use dough that's aged for at least three days:** There's tremendous flavor development over the first few days of storage.

VARIATION 1: HERB DOUGH

This simple recipe shows off the versatility of our approach. Herb-scented breads are great favorites for appetizers and snacks. Just follow the directions for mixing the Master Recipe and add 1 teaspoon dried thyme leaves (or 2 teaspoons fresh) and ½ teaspoon dried rosemary leaves (or 1 teaspoon fresh) to the water mixture. You can use herbs with any of the dough formulas in this book; it doesn't change the storage time.

VARIATION 2: OLIVE OIL DOUGH

Simply swap out ¼ cup of water for ¼ cup of oil. Olive oil adds richness and flavor in pizza (page 158), focaccia (page 163), and Olive Bread (page 120), but it's also great when used in any of the loaves in this chapter. It makes a more tender loaf with a delicious flavor (but tends not to create a crisp crust). For different flavor effects, try swapping in other oils, like safflower, avocado, grapeseed, or flaxseed, or melted butter. Coconut oil also works nicely, but it needs to be melted like butter. You can also do this with whole grain doughs, replacing ¼ cup of water with oil.

~

Amaze your friends with the "6-2-2-13" rule for a double-batch: If you want to store enough for seven to eight 1-pound loaves, here's a simple mnemonic for the recipe: 6, 2, 2, and 13. Combine 6 cups water, 2 tablespoons salt, and 2 tablespoons yeast; then mix in 13 cups of all-purpose flour. Store in a 10- to 12-quart lidded container. That's it. It will amaze your friends when you do this in their homes without a recipe—but tell them to buy this book anyway!

Amaze your friends even more with the 750/1,000 rule for a single batch measured with a metric scale: If you're measuring flour and water by metric weight, you can make a generous batch by weighing 1,000 grams of all-purpose flour and 750 grams of water. The yeast and salt don't need to change, but you can slightly increase the salt to account for the extra 90 grams of flour.

Whole wheat boules, page 79

Loaf breads, page 85

Bâtard shape with sesame seeds, page 94

Moon and Stars Bread, page 95

Baguette, page 88

Pain d'Épi (wheat stalk bread), page 92

Ciabatta, page 96

Couronne, page 98

Pita, page 100

Crock Pot Bread, page 105

Rolls, page 108

Rosemary Crescents, page 112

Garlic Knots with Parsley and Olive Oil, page 114

From bottom left, Olive Bread, page 120, Fougasse Stuffed with Roasted
Red Pepper, page 168, and Olive Fougasse, page 166

Pumpernickel Bread, page 125, Deli-Style Rye Bread, page 122

Black-and-White Braided Pumpernickel and Rye Loaf, page 128

Strong White Dough

When bakers talk about the "strength" of a dough, they're talking about the dough's firmness, resilience, and stretch, which results from the gluten (bread protein) in flour. Strong dough made with bread flour or other high-protein flours feels firmer in your hand and holds a shape better than dough made with all-purpose flour. It also creates the chewier crumb that characterizes bagels and pretzels (pages 146 and 150). Some of our readers prefer it for their loaf breads and pizza, and it works well for all of the loaves in this chapter, but especially for fancy shapes like Baguette (page 88), and Pain d'Épi (page 92). The flavor of malt is traditional in American bagels, so malt is an optional ingredient for those (it doesn't matter if you use diastatic or non-diastatic malt). **If you don't have bread flour, you can get a similar effect with all-purpose white flour, but increase to 6¾ cups (2 pounds, 2 ounces/955 grams).**

Makes four loaves, slightly less than 1 pound each. The recipe can be doubled or halved.

Ingredient	Volume (U.S.)	Weight (U.S.)	Weight (Metric)
Bread flour	6½ cups	2 pounds	910 grams
Granulated yeast*	1 tablespoon	0.35 ounce	10 grams
Kosher salt[1]	1 to 1½ tablespoons	0.6 to 0.9 ounce	17 to 25 grams
OPTIONAL, for bagels: Malt powder or sugar	2 tablespoons	1 ounce	30 grams
Lukewarm water (100°F or below)	3 cups	1 pound, 8 ounces	680 grams

[1]Can adjust to taste (see pages 18 and 20).

1. **Mixing and storing the dough:** Whisk together the flour, yeast, salt, (and malt powder or sugar, if using), in a 6-quart bowl, or a lidded (not airtight) food container.

2. Add the water and mix without kneading, using a spoon or a heavy-duty stand mixer (with the paddle/flat beater). You might need to use wet hands to get the last bit of flour to incorporate if you're not using a machine.

3. Cover (not airtight), and allow the dough to rest at room temperature until it rises and collapses (or flattens on top), approximately 2 hours.

4. The dough can be used immediately after the initial rise, though it is easier to handle when cold. Refrigerate it in a lidded (not airtight) container and use over the next 14 days; freeze (airtight) if you're keeping it longer than that.

6

MORE BASIC DOUGHS

In the pages that follow, you'll find more dough formulas that all work with Chapter 5's basic boule shape, with any of the classic shapes (pages 85–115), and with any of the flatbread or pizza recipes (pages 157–70).

100% Whole Wheat Dough

100% Whole Wheat Dough is particularly sensitive to the brand of flour used, so before trying this recipe, become familiar with how our basic white dough in Chapter 5 looks and feels, and be ready to vary the amount of water you use. Unlike our white-flour recipes, this one may require you to make adjustments on the fly, because whole wheat flour brands vary more than white flour.

Some of our tasters and testers preferred 100 percent whole grain loaves made with extra wheat gluten, which lightens the loaf and makes it airier (see Ingredients, page 13). But not everyone needs or wants the extra gluten, so check out Whole Wheat Variation 1, below, which omits it. **It's important to whisk vital wheat gluten into the dry ingredients before adding water; otherwise, clumps will form.**

Makes four loaves, slightly less than 1 pound each. The recipe can be doubled or halved.

Ingredient	Volume (U.S.)	Weight (U.S.)	Weight (Metric)
Whole wheat flour[1]	7²/₃ cups	2 pounds, 3 ounces	1,000 grams
Granulated yeast[2]	1 tablespoon	0.35 ounce	10 grams
Kosher salt[2]	1 to 1¹/₂ table-spoons	0.6 to 0.9 ounce	17 to 25 grams
Vital wheat gluten	¹/₄ cup	1³/₈ ounces	40 grams
Lukewarm water (100°F or below)	4¹/₄ cups	2 pounds, 2 ounces	965 grams

[1] Can substitute white whole wheat (see page 13).
[2] Can adjust to taste (see pages 18 and 20).

1. **Mixing and storing the dough:** Whisk together the flour, yeast, salt, and vital wheat gluten in a 6-quart bowl, or a lidded (not airtight) food container. (Vital wheat gluten will clump if you add it directly to water.)

2. Add the water and mix without kneading, using a spoon, or a heavy-duty stand mixer (with the paddle/flat beater). You might need to use wet hands to get the last bit of flour to incorporate if you're not using a machine.

3. Cover (not airtight), and allow the dough to rest at room temperature until it rises and collapses (or flattens on top), approximately 2 hours.

4. The dough can be used immediately after the initial rise, though it is easier to handle when cold. Refrigerate it in a lidded (not airtight)

container and use it over the next 5 days; freeze (airtight) if you're keeping it longer than that.

5. Use in any of the recipes calling for lean dough, including the Master Recipe and variations in Chapter 5 (same baking temperatures and times).

WHOLE WHEAT VARIATION 1: 100% WHOLE WHEAT DOUGH WITHOUT VITAL WHEAT GLUTEN

Omit the vital wheat gluten and decrease the water to 3¾ cups (1 pound, 14 ounces/850 grams). Depending on the brand of whole wheat you're using, you may have to adjust the water amount. Without vital wheat gluten, results will be denser, especially with storage, but still delicious. You can omit the vital wheat gluten with any of the following whole wheat variations as well. **Maximum storage duration before freezing:** 5 days.

WHOLE WHEAT VARIATION 2: 100% WHOLE GRAIN RYE DOUGH

You can swap out up to 1 cup of the whole wheat flour for rye in this rec-ipe—any more than that and you'll get a loaf that's too dense for most people, because rye doesn't have the gluten content of wheat. Caraway (1½ tablespoons) in the mixing water or whisked into the flour turns this into a whole grain deli-style rye (see page 122). **Maximum storage duration before freezing:** 5 days.

WHOLE WHEAT VARIATION 3: HONEY WHOLE WHEAT

Honey whole wheat is a classic American loaf, loved even by finicky eaters who object to whole grains. That's because the sugar in honey acts as a ten-derizer, and its mellow sweetness acts as a perfect foil to the slight bitter-ness of whole wheat. **Best of all, it's a simple variation:** Just put ½ cup honey (6 ounces/170 grams) into the liquid measuring cup, then top it off with water to the required amount, decrease the baking temperature to 350°F, and increase the baking time to 45 minutes (sweet loaves scorch at high temperatures). **Maximum storage duration before freezing:** 5 days.

WHOLE WHEAT VARIATION 4: 100% WHOLE WHEAT WITH OIL AND A LITTLE SWEETENER (THE TENDERIZING TEAM)

If your family shies from whole wheat bread because they like the softness and tenderness of white bread, here's the solution. A small amount of oil (or melted butter) plus sweetener tenderizes any whole grain bread. Just put 2 tablespoons each of oil (or melted unsalted butter) and honey into the liquids measuring cup, then top it off with water to the required amount. Because there's only a touch of sweetness, baking time and temperature remain the same. Sugar will work as well as honey (but adds no flavor boost); you can add 2 tablespoons with the dry ingredients. Other swaps for honey: malt syrup, maple syrup, molasses, or agave syrup. Each will impart its own flavor, with molasses making the strongest impression. **Maximum storage duration before freezing:** 5 days.

Light Whole Wheat Dough

You'll find this recipe a basic workhorse when you want a versatile and healthy light wheat bread for sandwiches, appetizers, and snacks. The blend of all-purpose flour and whole wheat creates a bread that is lighter in texture, taste, and appearance than our other whole grain breads.

Makes four loaves, slightly less than 1 pound each. The recipe can be doubled or halved.

Ingredient	Volume (U.S.)	Weight (U.S.)	Weight (Metric)
Lukewarm water (100°F or below)	3 cups	1 pound, 8 ounces	680 grams
Granulated yeast[1]	1 tablespoon	0.35 ounce	10 grams
Kosher salt[1]	1 to 1½ tablespoons	0.6 to 0.9 ounce	17 to 25 grams
Whole wheat flour[2]	1 cup	4½ ounces	130 grams
All-purpose flour	5½ cups	1 pound, 11½ ounces	780 grams

[1]Can adjust to taste (see pages 18 and 20).
[2]Can substitute white whole wheat (see page 13).

1. **Mixing and storing the dough:** Mix the yeast and salt with the water in a 6-quart bowl or a lidded (not airtight) food container.

2. Mix in the flours without kneading, using a spoon or a heavy-duty stand mixer (with the paddle/flat beater). If you're not using a machine, you may need to use wet hands to incorporate the last bit of flour.

3. Cover (not airtight) and allow to rest at room temperature until the dough rises and collapses (or flattens on top), approximately 2 hours.

4. The dough can be used immediately after the initial rise, though it is easier to handle when cold. Refrigerate the container of dough and use over the next 14 days.

5. Use in any of the recipes calling for lean dough, including the Master Recipe in Chapter 5. Whole grain loaves are gorgeous baked as boules (see color photo).

VARIATION: MORE WHOLE WHEAT

For a heartier, wheatier loaf, increase the water to 3⅛ cups (1 pound, 10 ounces/735 grams). Then, increase the whole wheat flour to 3 cups (13½ ounces/385 grams) and decrease the all-purpose flour to 3½ cups (1 pound, 1½ ounces/500 grams). **Maximum storage duration before freezing:** 10 days.

7

CLASSIC SHAPES WITH MASTER AND BASIC DOUGHS

Y ou can make any of these classic shapes using any of our white or whole grain doughs from Chapter 5 or Chapter 6. Enjoy!

Crusty and Hearty White Sandwich Loaf

This loaf is nothing like commercial white bread, that impossibly soft stuff best used for wadding up and tossing across lunchrooms. The crust is firm if not actually crackling. The stored dough adds sourdough complexity to a traditionally plain recipe, and the steam adds caramelization to the crust, proving that loaf breads can be as artfully beautiful as free-form ones (see color photo).

This variation will give you some experience baking high-moisture dough in a loaf pan. Nonstick pans release their contents more easily, but you can use a traditional loaf pan if it's heavy gauge and you grease it well; otherwise, it's likely to stick.

Makes 1 loaf
2 pounds (large cantaloupe–size portion) any Master, Basic, or European
  Peasant dough (pages 63–84, or 117)
Oil, for greasing the pan

1. Dust the surface of the refrigerated dough with flour and cut off a 2-pound (large cantaloupe–size) piece. Dust with more flour and quickly shape it into a ball by stretching the surface of the dough around to the bottom on all four sides, rotating the ball a quarter-turn as you go. Grease an 8½ × 4½-inch loaf pan with oil (grease heavily if you're not using a nonstick pan).

2. Elongate the ball into an oval and drop it into the prepared pan.

3. **Dust the top surface with a little flour, cover loosely with plastic wrap, and allow to rest for 90 minutes** (see sidebar, page 70). Dust with flour and slash the top crust with a serrated bread knife.

You don't necessarily have to slash breads baked in a pan: A loaf pan or a close-fitting cast-iron pot will prevent shape problems. The top crust may crack open randomly but the loaf won't be misshapen.

4. **Preheat the oven to 450°F,** with an empty metal broiler tray on any rack that won't interfere with the rising bread. A baking stone is not required, and omitting it shortens the preheat. If you're using a stone to even out the heating in your oven, preheat for 20 to 30 minutes, otherwise, 5 to 10 minutes is enough in most ovens.

5. Place on a rack in the center of the oven. Pour 1 cup of hot water into

the broiler tray and quickly close the oven door. Bake for about 45 minutes, or until brown and firm. To be sure there isn't underbaked dough in the center of the loaf, insert a thin-bladed knife or a temperature probe into the center of the loaf. It should come out clean.

6. Remove the loaf from the pan and allow to cool completely on a rack before slicing; otherwise you won't get well-cut slices.

VARIATION: A LOAF BREAD IMMEDIATELY AFTER MIXING
Immediately after mixing (before rising), transfer 2 pounds of dough directly into a greased loaf pan and allow to rest for 2 hours (or until the dough approximately doubles in volume). Bake as above.

Pro tips for loaf-pan breads:

- **If the loaf sticks,** wait 10 minutes and it will steam itself loose from the pan. Run a table knife around the loaf to dislodge any spots that still adhere, then grab a wide-bladed spatula to pry it out—often this is easier from the short end.

- **Slicing loaf-pan breads:** Here's a simple fix for uneven slices. First, let the loaf cool completely (it may take 2 hours). Use a good-quality bread knife (page 36) and a cutting board. **Turn the loaf upside down to slice, so that the knife bites against the sharply angled corner of the bottom of the loaf. If you start your cut against the domed top of the loaf, you'll get compressed, uneven slices.** This works for slicing any loaf bread.

Baguette

This is the quintessential thin and crusty loaf of France, served at every meal and the symbol of an entire cuisine. Baguettes are defined as much by their crust as their crumb; a crisp crust can make the loaf sensational (see color photo). Aside from the shaping, one important technique that differentiates the baguette from the boule in Chapter 5 is that the baguette is not heavily dusted with flour, at least not traditionally. So, to keep the knife from sticking, brush water onto the surface of the loaf just before slashing. You'll also notice that for this loaf we use whole wheat flour rather than cornmeal on the pizza peel, since cornmeal would impart too strong a flavor to classic baguettes (parchment paper's also a nice option).

Traditional recipes for baguettes are high-maintenance, so if you've done this the old-fashioned way, our approach should be a relief. A 20-minute rest after shaping is all that is needed to create a light and airy loaf. So our baguette is delicious, and very, very fast. Traditionally, this is a white loaf, but you can make it with whole grain dough as well.

Makes 1 baguette

½ pound (orange-size portion) any Master or Basic ("lean") dough (pages 63–84); Strong White Dough (page 77) will hold its shape better in this loaf

All-purpose flour, for dusting

Whole wheat flour or parchment paper, for the pizza peel

1. **Preheat a baking stone near the middle of the oven to 450°F (20 to 30 minutes),** with an empty broiler tray on any rack that won't interfere with the rising bread. **NOTE: In some ovens, you'll get a crisper, browner crust if you preheat the stone to 475°F and then turn it down to 450°F when you put the baguette into the oven. And a longer**

preheat may be beneficial for this traditionally very crisp bread (40 minutes or longer).

2. Dust the surface of the refrigerated dough with all-purpose flour and cut off a ½-pound (orange-size) piece. Dust with more flour and quickly shape it into a ball by stretching the surface of the dough around to the bottom on all four sides, rotating the ball a quarter-turn as you go. Once it's cohesive, begin to stretch and elongate the dough, dusting with additional flour as necessary. You may find it helpful to roll it back and forth with your hands on a flour-dusted surface. Form a cylinder approximately 1½ inches in diameter. Place the loaf on a pizza peel covered with whole wheat flour or parchment paper and allow to rest for 20 minutes (for professional shaping tips, see **the letter-fold technique on the next page**).

3. After the dough has rested, paint the loaf with water, using a pastry brush. Slash the loaf diagonally, using a serrated bread knife (see photo, page 91).

4. Slide the loaf directly onto the hot stone. Pour 1 cup of hot water into the broiler tray and quickly close the oven door (see page 28 for steam alternatives). Bake for about 25 minutes, or until deeply browned and firm to the touch.

5. Allow to cool on a rack before cutting.

The letter-fold technique—creating a perfect taper: Our simple stretch-and-roll method will give you a decent baguette, but you might not match the skinny taper achieved by professional bakers. Here's a more polished method—if you perfect this, yours will look just like the ones in the bakery window. In addition to using it for skinny baguettes, you can use the letter-fold to get professional tapered ends with your basic oval loaves, such as the Bâtard (page 94) or Deli-Style Rye Bread (page 122). **Here's what you do:**

1. Gently stretch the dough into a $1/2$-inch-thick oval. Fold in one of the long sides and gently press it into the center, taking care not to compress the dough too much.

2. Bring up the other side to the center and pinch the seam closed. This letter-fold technique puts less dough into the ends—that's what gives you the nice taper.

3. Stretch and roll very gently into a log, working the dough until you have a thin baguette. Again, try not to compress the air out of the dough. If the dough resists pulling, let it rest for 5 to 10 minutes to relax the gluten, then continue to stretch—don't fight the dough. You can continue to stretch lengthwise during the 20-minute rest, until you achieve the desired thin result, about $1^{1}/2$ inches wide.

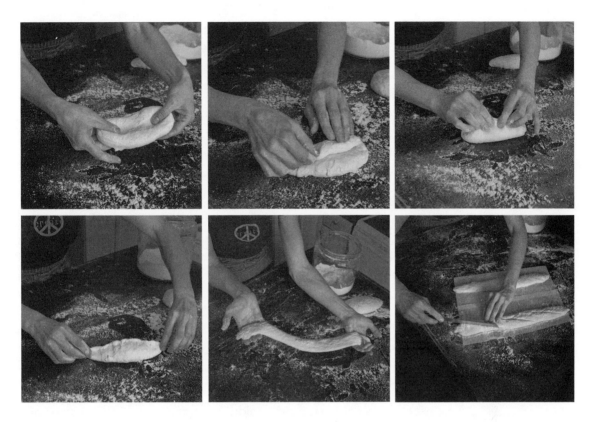

Pain d'Épi—Wheat Stalk Bread (pan deh-peé)

Fancifully shaped like a stalk of wheat with individual "grains," the pain d'épi is a simple yet impressive bread to present to guests (see color photo). To preserve the shape of those wheat grains, Strong White Dough (page 77), will help the pain d'épi hold its shape, but you'll get reasonable results with the other listed doughs as well (the charming "wheat grains" won't be so well defined).

Makes 1 pain d'épi

½ pound (orange-size portion) any Master or Basic ("lean") dough, pages 63–84. Strong White Dough (page 77) will hold its shape better in this loaf

All-purpose flour, for dusting

Parchment paper for the pizza peel

1. **Preheat a baking stone near the middle of the oven to 450°F (20 to 30 minutes),** with an empty metal broiler tray on any rack that won't interfere with the rising bread.

2. Dust the surface of the refrigerated dough with flour and cut off a ½-pound (orange-size) piece. Dust with more flour and quickly shape it into a ball by stretching the surface of the dough around to the bottom on all four sides, rotating the ball a quarter-turn as you go.

3. Using the letter-fold technique (see sidebar, page 90), form a slender baguette. You can skip the letter-fold, but the "grains" won't be as beautiful.

4. Lay the baguette on the edge of a prepared pizza peel. For this loaf, parchment paper is preferred because it will facilitate sliding it into the oven without distortion or sticking. Allow to rest for 20 minutes.

5. Dust the surface of the loaf with flour. Using kitchen shears and starting at one end of the loaf, cut into the dough at a very shallow angle. If you cut too vertically, the "wheat grains" won't be as pointy. Cut with a single snip to within ¼ inch of the work surface, but be careful not to cut all the way through the loaf or you'll have separate rolls (see photo).

6. As you cut, lay each piece over to alternate sides. Continue to cut until you've reached the end of the stalk (see photos).

7. Slide the loaf directly onto the hot stone, parchment paper and all. Pour 1 cup of hot water into the broiler tray and quickly close the oven door (see page 28 for steam alternatives). Bake for about 25 minutes, or until richly browned and firm. Removing the parchment for the last 10 minutes will help crisp the bottom crust.

5. Allow to cool on a rack before eating.

Bâtard (báh-tar)

The *bâtard*, a short and wide French shape with pointed ends, is more suitable to use for sandwiches than a baguette. If you like, you can make the bâtard almost as wide as a sandwich loaf, but traditionally it is about 3 inches across at its widest point. The bâtard is tapered to a point at each end. For a more perfectly shaped bâtard, you can use the letter-fold technique (see sidebar, page 90); just don't make it so skinny.

Makes 1 bâtard

   1 pound (grapefruit-size portion) any Master or Basic ("lean") dough,
      pages 63–84
   All-purpose flour, for dusting
   Sesame seeds, if desired

1. Follow steps 1 and 2 for the baguette on page 88, but shape the loaf to a diameter of about 3 inches (you can use the letter-fold technique on page 90 for a professional look).

2. When forming the loaf on the floured surface, concentrate pressure at the ends to form the bâtard's traditional taper.

3. Follow steps 3 through 5 for the baguette. Increase the resting time to 40 minutes, and the baking time to 30 minutes, or until deeply brown. Sesame seeds look beautiful on this shape, so paint with water and sprinkle with seeds just before baking, if desired (see color photo).

VARIATION:
MOON AND STARS BREAD

This whimsical and crusty traditional Italian shape maximizes surfaces exposed to the oven's crisping steam and browning heat, its caramelized surface contrasting beautifully with sesame seeds (see color photo). Shape a thinnish bâtard, as above, but taper the ends by rolling them between your palms and pinching them (the letter-fold technique is helpful here, and building your loaf on parchment helps preserve the fancy shape when you slide it into the oven). Bend the loaf into a semicircle—this will become your moon shape. Rest the loaf, then use a pastry brush to paint the loaf with water or cornstarch wash (see page 121), and sprinkle with sesame seeds. Then use kitchen shears to snip 1- to 2-inch-deep cuts into the bread on the outside of the curve. There's no need to slash this loaf. Bake as for a bâtard.

Ciabatta (cha-báh-tah)

The word *ciabatta* is Italian for "slipper," and refers to the shape of the bread, which is halfway between a flatbread and a loaf. It's made from very wet dough and shaped as an elongated oval or rectangle—perhaps you have slippers shaped like this? (see color photo). To achieve the very moist crumb, shape the loaf with wet hands rather than dusting with flour. The bread will be chewy and moist, with large and appealing air holes, especially if you use longer-aged dough. Ciabatta is baked without cornmeal on the bottom, so dust the pizza peel with an ample coating of white flour instead. And, since white flour is a less efficient "stick-preventer" than cornmeal, you may need to nudge the loaf off the peel with a steel dough scraper or spatula (or use parchment paper).

Makes 1 ciabatta

1 pound (grapefruit-size portion) any Master, Basic, or European
    Peasant dough (pages 63–84, or 117)
All-purpose flour or parchment paper, for the pizza peel

1. Cut off a 1-pound (grapefruit-size) piece of refrigerated dough without dusting the surface with flour; wet hands will help prevent sticking. Using your wet hands, shape the dough into a ball by stretching the surface of the dough around to the bottom on all four sides, rotating the ball a quarter-turn as you go. With your wet fingers, flatten the ball into an elongated oval about ¾ inch thick. If you make it much thinner, it may puff like pita bread, which isn't desirable here.

2. **Preheat a baking stone near the middle of the oven to 450°F (20 to 30 minutes),** with an empty metal broiler tray on any rack that won't interfere with the rising bread.

3. Place the loaf on a pizza peel covered with flour or parchment paper and allow to rest for 20 minutes (increase to 40 minutes if you're not getting the large hole structure you want). Dust the top with flour, but don't slash the loaf.

4. Slide the loaf directly onto the hot stone, using a steel dough scraper or spatula to nudge it off if it sticks (this won't be necessary if you're using parchment paper; just slide off onto the stone, paper and all). Pour 1 cup of hot water into the broiler tray and quickly close the oven door (see page 28 for steam alternatives). If you notice puffing through the oven door, poke the air bubbles with a long-handled fork. Bake for 20 to 25 minutes, or until deeply brown.

5. Allow to cool on a rack before cutting or eating.

Couronne (cor-ówn)

This ring, or crown-shaped French loaf, is a specialty of Lyon. The couronne is quite simple to shape and is a beautiful alternative to the classic boule (see color photo).

Makes 1 couronne

1 pound (grapefruit-size portion) any Master, Basic, or European Peasant dough (pages 63–84, or 117)
All-purpose flour, for dusting
Whole wheat flour, cornmeal, or parchment paper, for the pizza peel

1. **Preheat a baking stone near the middle of the oven to 450°F (20 to 30 minutes),** with an empty metal broiler tray on any rack that won't interfere with the rising bread.

2. Dust the surface of the refrigerated dough with all-purpose flour and cut off a 1-pound (grapefruit-size) piece. Dust the piece with more flour and quickly shape it into a ball by stretching the surface of the dough around to the bottom on all four sides, rotating the ball a

quarter-turn as you go. When a cohesive ball has formed, poke your thumbs through the center of the ball and gradually stretch the hole so that it is about three times as wide as the wall of the ring; otherwise, the hole will close up during baking.

3. Place the loaf on a pizza peel covered with flour, cornmeal, or parchment paper and allow to rest for 20 minutes.

4. Dust the couronne with flour and slash radially, like spokes in a wheel.

5. Slide the loaf directly onto the hot stone. Pour 1 cup of hot water into the broiler tray and quickly close the oven door (see page 28 for steam alternatives). Bake for 25 to 30 minutes, or until deeply browned and firm. (Smaller or larger loaves will require adjustments in baking time.)

6. Allow the bread to cool before cutting or eating.

Pita

Pita bread is the puffy, flour-dusted "pocket" flatbread of the Middle East (see color photo). It is a simple and elemental bread and, for reasons we can't explain, it's just about our most fragrant one. Aside from being delicious, this bread is among the fastest in the book to make. It's easy to produce beautiful puffed loaves. The secret to the puffing (pocketing) is to roll the dough thinly and use a hot oven with a stone. Because pita isn't slashed, steam is trapped inside. As soon as the top and bottom crusts set, steam in the interior pushes them apart. Pita is delicious warm from the oven—unlike loaf breads, it doesn't need to cool completely.

"Because pita is so fast and easy, it became the true daily bread for my kids' lunches when they were growing up. We made it every morning before school."

—Jeff

Makes one 12-inch pita, or 2 small individual pitas

½ pound (orange-size portion) any Master, Basic, or European Peasant dough (pages 63–84, or 117)
All purpose flour, for dusting
Flour or parchment paper, for the pizza peel

1. **Preheat a baking stone to 500°F (20 to 30 minutes).** You won't be using a broiler tray and rack placement of the stone is not crucial. Prepare a pizza peel with flour or parchment paper.

2. Dust the surface of the refrigerated dough with flour and cut off a ½-pound (orange-size) piece. Dust the piece with more flour and quickly shape it into a ball by stretching the surface of the dough around to the bottom on all four sides, rotating the ball a quarter-turn as you go.

3. Using your hands and a rolling pin, roll the dough into a round with a uniform thickness of $\frac{1}{8}$ inch throughout—if it's too thick, it won't puff. Sprinkle the work surface lightly with flour to prevent sticking to the rolling pin or to the board, occasionally flipping the pita as you work. Use a dough scraper to dislodge the pita if it sticks, and drop the pita on the prepared pizza peel. No resting time is needed. Do not slash the pita or it will not puff.

> ∽
>
> **Troubleshooting pita that won't puff:**
>
> The two likeliest solutions:
>
> - **Too thick?** Roll it thinner, making sure to achieve $\frac{1}{8}$-inch thickness.
>
> - **Not hot enough?** Make sure your oven's up to temperature, checking with an oven thermometer (see page 32). A longer oven preheat of the stone may help, so consider trying 45 or 60 minutes if you're not getting the puffing you'd like.

4. Place the tip of the peel near the back of the stone, close to where you want the far edge of the pita to land. Give the peel a few quick forward-and-back jiggles and pull it sharply out from under the pita. Bake for 6 to 8 minutes, or until lightly browned and puffed. You may need to transfer the pita to a higher rack (without the stone) to achieve browning. Don't over-bake or you risk dryness.

5. For the most authentic, soft-crusted pita, wrap in a clean cotton dish towel and set on a cooling rack when baking is complete. The pita will deflate slightly as it cools. The space between crusts will still be there, but may have to be nudged apart with a fork.

6. Serve the pita as a sandwich pocket. Once the pita is cool, store in a plastic bag. Unlike hard-crusted breads, pita is not harmed by airtight storage.

VARIATION 1: PITA BREAD MADE UNDER THE BROILER

If you don't have time to heat up a baking stone, just use the broiler. Prepare a heavy-gauge baking sheet, pizza pan, or cast-iron skillet with oil (if your pan is well seasoned and the dough is well dusted, you can use minimal oil, or even none at all). Stretch your pita as above, put it into the pan, and broil 4 to 5 inches from the heat source for about 3 minutes, or until puffy and browned. Turn over and continue for about 3 more minutes. The pita will slightly collapse with turning and may singe in places.

VARIATION 2: PITA BREAD ON THE STOVETOP (UNLIKELY TO PUFF!)

Prepare the pita as above, then heat a heavy 12-inch skillet (cast-iron works great) over high heat on the stovetop. Add 2 tablespoons of oil and drop the dough into the pan (you can use less oil for a different effect, if you're sure to keep the dough-round well dusted or if your pan is nonstick). Decrease the heat to medium and cover the skillet to trap steam and heat. Check for doneness with a spatula at 3 minutes (sooner if you're smelling scorching), adjusting the flame as needed. Flip when the underside is richly browned and continue for another 2 to 6 minutes, until the bread feels firm throughout. **If you use ghee (Indian-style clarified butter), you'll get something closer to naan.** It won't quite be authentic since you probably don't have an authentic Indian tandoor oven, but the ghee re-creates some of the flavors of that distinctive flatbread.

Baba Ghanoush: A Fantastic Middle Eastern Eggplant Spread for Pita

"In our pizza and flatbread book, we included a baba ghanoush recipe that relied on charring the eggplant under the broiler, and then peeling and discarding the charred skin, which, though traditional, is slow and tedious. I discovered an easy shortcut—just slow-roast the eggplants until well browned, but not charred, and then food-process the whole thing, including the skin. The browning creates the same wonderful smoky flavor without all that hassle and waste." —Jeff

Makes about 3 cups dip

Olive oil, for greasing the pan

4 eggplants (small skinny ones are best; big ones will take much longer to roast)

Juice of 2 lemons and their zest (removed with a microplane zester; see page 38)

4 large raw garlic cloves, or to taste, coarsely chopped (variation: 4 roasted garlic cloves, chopped or mashed, see the next page)

¾ cup tahini paste

½ teaspoon kosher salt

1. Preheat the oven to 400°F. Grease a rimmed baking sheet with olive oil. Pierce the eggplants in several places with a sharp knife to prevent bursting.

2. Place the eggplants on the greased rimmed baking sheet and roast, turning occasionally, until the skin is well browned and the flesh is very soft, about 40 minutes, depending on the size of the eggplants. Set aside to cool and reserve any juice that runs into the pan.

3. When cooled, cut the eggplants into chunks that your food processor can handle. Run all the ingredients through the food processor until smooth, but hold back the reserved liquid, adding enough to produce a smooth dip, and adding water or olive oil if needed.

4. Serve with pita and refrigerate for up to 1 week.

Roasted garlic cloves: Wrap the garlic, unpeeled, in aluminum foil and bake for 30 minutes at 400°F. Allow to cool, then peel. Or, cut across the top of each clove and squeeze out the soft roasted garlic pulp.

Crock Pot Bread (Fast Bread in a Slow Cooker)

Everyone loves crock pots, bubbling away with Swedish meatballs, no-peek chicken, or chili. Over the years we got requests for a method for baking our dough in one. **Bread in a crock pot? We had our doubts, lots of them.** We didn't think a slow cooker could get hot enough; thought it would take too long; didn't think it would bake through or have a nice crust. So we resisted trying it, convinced it would fail. **Oh, how wrong we were** (see color photo). The crock pot does indeed get hot enough, and it takes less time than using your oven because the rising time is included in the baking. Straight out of the pot, the crust is soft and pale, but a few minutes under the broiler gives you a gorgeous loaf. In the summer there is no need to heat up the oven to get great bread, and at holiday times it frees up much-needed oven space. You can even amaze your friends at work by baking a loaf under your desk.

Makes 1 loaf

   1 pound (grapefruit-size portion) any Master, Basic, or European Peasant
      dough (pages 63–84, or 117)
   All-purpose flour, for dusting
   Parchment paper, for baking

1. Dust the surface of the refrigerated dough with flour and cut off a
    1-pound (grapefruit-size) piece. Dust with more flour and quickly
    shape it into a ball by stretching the surface of the dough around to the
    bottom on all four sides, rotating the ball a quarter-turn as you go.
    Place it on a sheet of parchment paper.

2. Lower the dough into a 4-quart crock pot or other slow cooker. Be
    sure to follow the manufacturer's instructions for proper use.

3. Turn the temperature to high and put on the cover. **(Not all crock pots behave the same, so you should keep an eye on the loaf after about 45 minutes to make sure it is not over-browning on the bottom or not browning at all. You may need to adjust the time according to your appliance.)**

4. Bake for 1 hour (this will depend on your crock pot; you may need to increase or decrease the time). **Check for doneness;** it should feel firm when you gently poke the top of the loaf.

5. The bottom crust should be crisp, but the top of the loaf will be quite soft. Some folks desire a softer crust, so they'll love this loaf. But if you want a darker or crisper crust . . .

ᘒᘎ

Check with your crock pot's manufacturer: Some models' instructions specify that the crock pot has to be at least partially filled with a liquid to avoid safety or durability problems, so you can't use those brands. And never bake bread in a crock pot unattended.

6. Position a rack in the center of the oven and turn on the broiler. Remove the parchment paper and place the bread under the broiler for 5 minutes or until it browns.

7. **Let the loaf cool completely before slicing.** Cutting into a hot loaf is tempting, but it won't slice well and may seem gummy if you break into it before it's cooled—this is always true with high-moisture dough, but especially with loaves baked in a closed space—crock pots don't dissipate moisture as well as a regular oven does.

Soft Dinner Rolls, Baguette Buns, Brötchen, Cloverleaf Rolls, and Rosemary Crescents

Rolls are a delight to bake and adorable to look at (see color photo). They're small, so they need very little resting time before they go into the oven. And they don't have to cool completely like larger loaves do—it's okay to eat them slightly warm. You can make any of the following recipes with the Master Recipe, or try these easy shapes with other lean doughs, or even the enriched doughs for Challah (page 187) or Brioche (page 195), which yield softer rolls. **Be sure to decrease the oven temperature to 350°F when using egg-enriched dough, and increase baking time about 25 percent.**

Makes five 3-ounce rolls

> 1 pound (grapefruit-size portion) any Master, Basic, or European Peasant dough (pages 63–84, or 117), or Egg White–Enriched Brötchen dough (see sidebar, page 111)
> All-purpose flour, for dusting
> Egg white, for glazing the brötchen
> Melted unsalted butter or oil, for brushing the dinner rolls
> Unsalted butter, oil, or parchment paper, for the baking sheet

Soft Dinner Rolls

1. Preheat a baking stone near the middle of the oven to 450°F (20 to 30 minutes).

2. Cut off 3-ounce (small peach–size) pieces of Master Recipe dough and quickly shape into balls. Place the dough balls 2 inches apart on a baking sheet lined with parchment paper or a silicone mat and allow to rest for 20 minutes.

3. Cut a cross into the top of each roll, using a serrated knife or kitchen shears and keeping the shears perpendicular to the work surface when you cut.

4. Brush the tops with melted butter or oil and place the baking sheet in the oven. Bake for about 25 minutes, or until richly browned.

5. For the softest result, brush with more butter or oil. Serve slightly warm.

To make soft pull-apart rolls: Cut off a 1-pound (grapefruit-size) piece of Challah (page 187), Brioche (page 195), or Buttermilk Cinnamon-Raisin Bread dough (page 143), then divide the dough into 8 pieces and quickly shape them into balls. Place the dough balls in a greased 8 × 8-inch baking dish; they should be touching. Rest for 30 minutes. Preheat the oven to 350°F. Brush the tops of the rolls with melted butter before and after they go into the oven. Bake for about 30 minutes, or until golden brown. Serve slightly warm.

Baguette Buns

1. **Preheat a baking stone near the middle of the oven to 450°F (20 to 30 minutes),** with an empty metal broiler tray on any other rack.

2. Form a ½-pound baguette (see page 88) on a work surface; this will make about 6 buns. Using

a dough scraper or a knife, make angled parallel cuts about 2 inches apart along the length of the baguette to form rolls. Allow them to rest, 2 inches apart, on a baking sheet prepared with butter, oil, parchment paper, or a silicone mat for 20 minutes.

3. Place the baking sheet in the oven, pour 1 cup of hot water into the broiler tray, and quickly close the oven door (see page 28 for steam alternatives). Bake the rolls for about 25 minutes, or until richly browned. Serve slightly warm.

Brötchen (bro-chin)

On our website, people asked for German-style hard rolls, so we've included the most common: *brötchen* (German for "little bread"). They're traditionally made from dough enriched with egg whites and then brushed with more egg white before baking at high temperature with steam. The egg white creates an incredible crust and crumb—see the sidebar on the next page for an easy variation that turns the Master Recipe into brötchen dough for superb hard rolls.

1. **Preheat the oven to 450°F,** with an empty metal broiler tray on any rack that won't interfere with the rising brötchen.

2. Cut off 3-ounce (small peach–size) pieces of **Egg White–Enriched Dough for Brötchen** (see next page) and quickly shape into balls, then pinch to form an oval shape. Place the dough balls 2 inches apart, on a baking sheet prepared with oil, butter, parchment paper, or a silicone mat, and allow to rest for 20 minutes.

3. Brush the tops with egg white and cut a single lengthwise slash into the top of each roll, using a serrated knife.

4. Place the baking sheet in the oven, pour 1 cup of hot water into the broiler tray, and quickly close the oven door (see page 28 for steam alternatives). Bake the rolls for about 25 minutes, or until richly browned. Serve slightly warm.

∎

Egg white-enriched dough for brötchen: Put 3 egg whites in a 4-cup liquid measuring cup, then add water to bring the total volume to 3 cups of liquid. Substitute for the water in the Master Recipe (page 63), keeping all other ingredient measurements the same. Refrigerate the dough for up to 5 days before freezing in 1-pound portions. This dough is great for brötchen but you can use it for other rolls or bread as well.

Cloverleaf Rolls

1. **Preheat a baking stone near the middle of the oven to 450°F (20 to 30 minutes),** with an empty metal broiler tray on any other rack. Grease a muffin pan.

2. Cut off 3-ounce (small peach–size) pieces of dough. Cut each of these pieces into 4 smaller pieces. Shape each one into a smooth ball. Put the 4 balls together to form the cloverleaf and place in a cup of the prepared muffin pan. Continue with the remaining dough. Allow to rest for 30 minutes.

3. Slide the muffin pan into the oven, pour 1 cup of hot water into the broiler tray, and quickly close the oven door (see page 28 for steam alternatives). Bake for about 25 minutes, or until richly browned. Serve slightly warm.

Rosemary Crescents (see color photo)

½ pound (orange-size portion) any Master, Basic, or European Peasant dough (pages 63–84, or 117)
All-purpose flour, for dusting
3 tablespoons olive oil
½ teaspoon kosher salt
2 tablespoons finely chopped fresh rosemary or other herbs

1. Prepare a baking sheet with parchment paper, butter, oil, or a silicone mat.

2. Dust the surface of the refrigerated dough with flour and cut off a ½-pound (orange-size portion). Dust with more flour and quickly shape it into a ball by stretching the surface of the dough around to the bottom on all four sides, rotating the ball a quarter-turn as you go.

With a rolling pin, roll out the dough into a ⅛-inch-thick round. As you roll out the dough, use enough flour to prevent it from sticking to the work surface but not so much as to make the dough dry.

3. Spread 2 tablespoons of the olive oil over the dough and then sprinkle evenly with the salt and rosemary. Using a pizza cutter or a sharp knife, cut the dough into 8 equal-sized wedges, like a pizza.

4. Starting at the wider end, roll each wedge until the point is tucked securely under the bottom. Place rolls on baking sheet. Bend the ends in slightly to create the crescent shape. Brush the tops with the remaining olive oil and cover loosely with plastic wrap. Allow to rest about 40 minutes.

5. **Preheat the oven to 450°F.** A baking stone is not required, and omitting it shortens the preheat.

6. Bake for about 25 minutes, until golden brown and well set in the center.

Garlic Knots with Parsley and Olive Oil

Olive oil is our favorite oil flavor, and here's a recipe that really showcases it, using white, whole grain, or rye dough. Olive oil is rich in healthy monounsaturated fat, and is an authentically Italian way to enrich bread. Combined with parsley, garlic, and Parmigiano-Reggiano cheese, it's the essence of Mediterranean food (see color photo).

Makes 5 garlic knots

½ cup finely minced fresh flat-leaf parsley
4 garlic cloves, finely minced
¼ cup (2 ounces/55 grams) extra-virgin olive oil, plus more if needed
1 pound (grapefruit-size portion) any Master, Basic, or European Peasant
    dough (pages 63–84, or 117)
All-purpose flour, for dusting
1 tablespoon grated Parmigiano-Reggiano cheese

1. In a skillet, sauté the parsley and garlic in the olive oil for about 4 minutes over medium heat, until the garlic is soft and the mixture is aromatic. Add more olive oil if the mixture looks too dry, because you'll need to be able to drizzle this over the knots.

2. Dust the surface of the refrigerated dough with flour and divide the dough into five 3-ounce pieces (about the size of small peaches). Dust each piece with more flour and quickly shape into a ball by stretching the surface of the dough around to the bottom on all four sides, rotating each ball a quarter-turn as you go.

3. Elongate each ball into a rope a little less than ½ inch in diameter and tie it into a knot. Allow the knots to rest for 30 minutes, loosely

covered with plastic wrap or an overturned bowl, on an olive oil–greased baking sheet, or a baking sheet lined with a silicone mat or parchment paper.

4. **Preheat the oven to 425°F.** Place an empty metal broiler tray for holding water on any rack that won't interfere with the rising knots.

5. Drizzle the knots with three-quarters of the olive oil, garlic, and parsley mixture. Sprinkle the grated cheese over the knots.

6. Place the baking sheet on the middle rack in the oven, pour 1 cup of hot water into the broiler tray, and quickly close the oven door (see page 28 for steam alternatives). Bake for about 25 minutes, or until browned and firm. Drizzle the remaining olive oil mixture over the hot knots. Serve slightly warm.

8

LOAVES FROM AROUND
THE WORLD

With just a few tweaks, our basic doughs create classic bread styles from France, Italy, Germany, Britain, Eastern Europe, and, of course, the United States.

European Peasant Bread

The round, whole grain, country-style loaves of rural France (*pain de campagne*) and Italy (*pane rustica*) were once viewed as too rustic for stylish European tables—white flour was once an almost unattainable luxury. Today everyone enjoys the crackling crust and moist chewy crumb that define this peasant bread—the touches of whole wheat and rye make all the difference. Try this bread with anchovies, a strong cheese, and a hearty fish soup with lots of garlic and fresh herbs. It also bakes well as a loaf bread (page 85).

"This is the bread I would take to a desert island." —Jeff

Makes four loaves, slightly less than 1 pound each. The recipe is easily doubled or halved.

Ingredient	Volume (U.S.)	Weight (U.S.)	Weight (Metric)
Lukewarm water (100°F or below)	3 cups	1 pound, 8 ounces	680 grams
Granulated yeast[1]	1 tablespoon	0.35 ounce	10 grams
Kosher salt[1]	1 to 1½ table-spoons	0.6 to 0.9 ounce	17 to 25 grams
Rye flour	½ cup	2⅛ ounces	60 grams
Whole wheat flour	½ cup	2¼ ounces	65 grams
All-purpose flour	5½ cups	1 pound, 11½ ounces	780 grams
Cornmeal or parchment paper, for the pizza peel			

[1]Can adjust to taste (see pages 18 and 20).

1. **Mixing and storing the dough:** Mix the yeast and salt with the water in a 6-quart bowl or a lidded (not airtight) food container.

2. Mix in the remaining ingredients without kneading, using a spoon or a heavy-duty stand mixer (with the paddle/flat beater). If you're not using a machine, you may need to use wet hands to incorporate the last bit of flour.

3. Cover (not airtight) and allow to rest at room temperature until the dough rises and collapses (or flattens on top), approximately 2 hours.

4. The dough can be used immediately after the initial rise, though it is easier to handle when cold. Refrigerate the container of dough and use over the next 14 days. Freeze (airtight) if you're keeping it longer than that.

5. Dust the surface of the refrigerated dough with flour and cut off a 1-pound (grapefruit-size) piece. Dust with more flour and quickly shape it into a ball by stretching the surface of the dough around to the bottom on all four sides, rotating the ball a quarter-turn as you go. Place the loaf on a pizza peel prepared with cornmeal or parchment paper and allow to rest for 40 minutes (see sidebar, page 70).

6. **Preheat a baking stone near the middle of the oven to 450°F (20 to 30 minutes),** with an empty metal broiler tray on any rack that won't interfere with the rising bread. Sprinkle liberally with flour and slash the top, about ½ inch deep, using a serrated bread knife (see photos, page 71).

7. Slide the loaf directly onto the hot stone. Pour 1 cup of hot water into the broiler tray and quickly close the oven door (see page 28 for steam alternatives). Bake for about 35 minutes, or until richly browned and firm. (Smaller or larger loaves will require adjustments in resting and baking time.)

8. Allow to cool on a rack before slicing and eating.

Olive Bread

This bread is associated with the countries of the Mediterranean, especially Italy, France, and Spain, where olives are abundant and have incredible flavor (see color photo). Use the best-quality olives you can find; the wetter Kalamata variety work as well as the dry, salty Niçoise type, so it's your choice. The rich flavors of the olives make this a perfect accompaniment to cheeses, pasta tossed with fresh tomatoes, and other Mediterranean appetizers. We usually use black olives, but readers have told us that green ones are great, too.

This recipe is a great showcase for the versatility of our basic doughs, introducing a technique for rolling flavorful ingredients into a single loaf if you want to add variety and zest. But if you want a whole batch of olive dough, just mix a cup of halved olives into the initial mix of any of the doughs that we list.

Makes 1 loaf

1 pound (grapefruit-size portion) any Master, Basic, or European Peasant dough (pages 63–84, or 117)

All-purpose flour, for dusting

¼ cup high-quality olives, pitted and halved

Cornmeal or parchment paper, for the pizza peel

Cornstarch wash (see sidebar, opposite) or water, for brushing the loaf

1. Dust the surface of the refrigerated dough with flour and cut off a 1-pound (grapefruit-size) piece. Using your hands and a rolling pin,

flatten the dough to a thickness of ½ inch. Cover with the olives and roll up to seal inside the dough. Crimp the ends shut and tuck them under to form an oval loaf. Place the loaf on a pizza peel prepared with cornmeal or parchment paper, cover with plastic wrap or an overturned bowl, and allow to rest for 90 minutes.

2. **Preheat a baking stone near the middle of the oven to 450°F (20 to 30 minutes),** with an empty metal broiler tray on any rack that won't interfere with the rising bread.

Cornstarch wash: Using a fork, blend ½ teaspoon cornstarch with a small amount of water to form a paste. Add ½ cup water and whisk with a fork. Microwave or boil until the mixture appears glassy, about 30 to 60 seconds on high. It will keep in the refrigerator for two weeks. Traditional recipes tout cornstarch wash as a way to give shine to savory loaves, but we find it mainly adds flavor to the crust.

3. Paint the surface of the loaf with cornstarch wash or water, and slash the top, about ½ inch deep, using a serrated bread knife (see photos, page 71).

4. Slide the loaf directly onto the hot stone. Pour 1 cup of hot water into the broiler tray and quickly close the oven door (see page 28 for steam alternatives). Bake for about 35 minutes, or until the top crust is richly browned and firm. (Smaller or larger loaves will require adjustments in resting and baking time.)

5. Allow to cool on a rack before slicing and eating.

Deli-Style Rye Bread

Here's our version of a classic sourdough rye, which started Jeff's thirty-year obsession with bread baking (see color photo). Storing dough made with rye flour produces traditional flavor that rivals loaves made with a true sourdough starter (see page 231 if you want to try one). It's terrific on day one of the batch, but will be even better on day two or three, and will develop more sourdough flavor over the life of the batch. Traditionally it's glazed with cornstarch wash or water, which anchors the caraway and allows the slashing knife to pass through without sticking. The cornstarch-wash version adds flavor and color to the crust. Caraway seeds are so central to the classic rye bread flavor that many people think that its flavor is coming from the rye grain.

"My grandmother truly believed that this bread was better than cake. It turns out that elder immigrants from all over the world felt the same way about 'a good piece of bread.' Friends of Dutch and Scandinavian heritage remember older relatives shunning ordinary desserts in favor of extraordinary bread."

—Jeff

Makes 4 loaves, slightly less than 1 pound each. The recipe can be doubled or halved.

Ingredient	Volume (U.S.)	Weight (U.S.)	Weight (Metric)
Lukewarm water (100°F or below)	3 cups	1 pound, 8 ounces	680 grams
Granulated yeast[1]	1 tablespoon	0.35 ounce	10 grams
Caraway seeds (or try unconventional seeds, see page 23)	1½ tablespoons, plus additional for sprinkling the top	0.35 ounce	10 grams

Kosher salt[1]	1 to 1½ tablespoons	0.6 to 0.9 ounce	17 to 25 grams
Rye flour	1 cup	4¼ ounces	120 grams
All-purpose flour	5½ cups	1 pound, 11½ ounces	780 grams
Cornmeal or parchment paper, for the pizza peel			
Cornstarch wash (see sidebar, page 121) or water, for brushing the top crust			

[1]Can adjust to taste (see pages 18 and 20).

1. **Mixing and storing the dough:** Mix the yeast, caraway seeds, and salt with the water in a 6-quart bowl or a lidded (not airtight) food container.

2. Mix in the flours without kneading, using a spoon or a heavy-duty stand mixer (with the paddle/flat beater). If you're not using a machine, you may need to use wet hands to incorporate the last bit of flour.

3. Cover (not airtight) and allow to rest at room temperature until the dough rises and collapses (or flattens on top), approximately 2 hours.

4. The dough can be used immediately after the initial rise, though it is easier to handle when cold. Refrigerate the container of dough and use over the next 14 days. Freeze (airtight) if you're keeping it longer than that.

5. Dust the surface of the refrigerated dough with flour and cut off a 1-pound (grapefruit-size) piece. Dust the piece with more flour and quickly shape it into a ball by stretching the surface of the dough

around to the bottom on all four sides, rotating the ball a quarter-turn as you go. Elongate the ball to form an oval loaf—do it roughly or use the letter-fold technique (see sidebar, page 90). Place the loaf on a pizza peel prepared with cornmeal or parchment paper and allow to rest for 40 minutes (see sidebar, page 70).

6. **Preheat a baking stone near the middle of the oven to 450°F (20 to 30 minutes),** with an empty metal broiler tray on any rack that won't interfere with the rising bread.

7. Using a pastry brush, paint the top crust with cornstarch wash or water and then sprinkle with additional caraway seeds. Slash with ½-inch-deep parallel cuts across the loaf, using a serrated bread knife (see photos, page 71).

8. Slide the loaf directly onto the hot stone. Pour 1 cup of hot water into the broiler tray and quickly close the oven door (see page 28 for steam alternatives). Bake for 30 to 35 minutes, or until deeply browned and firm. (Smaller or larger loaves will require adjustments in baking time.)

9. Allow to cool on a rack before slicing and eating.

Pumpernickel Bread

Pumpernickel bread is traditional in Germany and Eastern Europe. It's really just a variety of rye bread (see color photo). What darkens the loaf and accounts for its mildly bitter but appealing flavor is powdered caramel coloring, cocoa, molasses, and coffee, not the flour. The caramel color is actually a natural ingredient made by overheating sugar until it is completely caramelized (available as a powder from King Arthur Baking Company; see Sources for Bread-Baking Products, page 243, or see the sidebar on page 127, to make your own liquid version). Traditional recipes use pumpernickel flour (a coarse rye with a lot of rye bran), but this grain doesn't do well in our recipes because it absorbs water unpredictably. Since it's really the caramel, coffee, and chocolate that give pumpernickel its unique flavor and color, we successfully created a pumpernickel bread without pumpernickel flour.

This bread is associated with Eastern Europe, where it's eaten with caviar. You could do the same or just pile on the pastrami and corned beef.

Makes 4 loaves, slightly less than 1 pound each. The recipe can be doubled or halved.

Ingredient	Volume (U.S.)	Weight (U.S.)	Weight (Metric)
Lukewarm water (100°F or below)	3 cups	1 pound, 8 ounces	680 grams
Granulated yeast[1]	1 tablespoon	0.35 ounce	10 grams
Kosher salt[1]	1 to 1½ tablespoons	0.6 to 0.9 ounce	17 to 25 grams
Molasses	2 tablespoons	1¼ ounces	35 grams

Cocoa powder, unsweetened	1½ tablespoons	0.4 ounce	10 grams
Instant espresso or instant coffee powder[2]	2 teaspoons	—	—
Caramel color	1½ tablespoons	—	—
Rye flour	1 cup	4¼ ounces	120 grams
All-purpose flour	5½ cups	1 pound, 11½ ounces	780 grams
Cornmeal or parchment paper, for the pizza peel			
Cornstarch wash (see sidebar, page 121) or water, for brushing the loaf			
Whole caraway seeds for sprinkling on the top (optional)			

[1]Can adjust to taste (see pages 18 and 20).
[2]Can substitute brewed coffee for 2 cups of the water, keeping total volume at 3 cups, omitting instant espresso or coffee powder.

1. **Mixing and storing the dough:** Mix the yeast, salt, molasses, cocoa, espresso powder, and caramel color with the water in a 6-quart bowl or a lidded (not airtight) food container.

2. Mix in the flours without kneading, using a spoon or a heavy-duty stand mixer (with the paddle/flat beater). If you're not using a machine, you may need to use wet hands to incorporate the last bit of flour.

3. Cover (not airtight) and allow to rest at room temperature until the dough rises and collapses (or flattens on top), approximately 2 hours.

4. The dough can be used immediately after the initial rise, though it is easier to handle when cold. Refrigerate the container of dough and use

over the next 8 days. Freeze (airtight) if you're keeping it longer than that.

5. Cut off a 1-pound (grapefruit-size) piece of dough. Using wet hands (don't use flour), quickly shape the dough into a ball by stretching the surface of the dough around to the bottom on all four sides, rotating the ball a quarter-turn as you go. Then form an oval-shaped loaf. Place the loaf on a pizza peel prepared with cornmeal or parchment paper and allow to rest for 40 minutes (see sidebar, page 70).

ᏏᎧ

Make your own caramel color: Caramel color can be made at home, but as a liquid rather than a powder. Put 3 tablespoons sugar and 1 tablespoon water into a saucepan. Over low heat, melt the sugar, then increase the heat to medium-high, cover, and bring to a boil for 2 minutes. Add a pinch of cream of tartar and continue to boil, uncovered, until the mixture becomes very dark. It will start to smoke at this point. Remove from the heat and allow to cool partially. Very carefully, add $1/2$ cup boiling water to the pan to dissolve the caramelized sugar (it may sputter and water may jump out of the pan, so wear gloves and be sure to shield your face). Cool to room temperature and use about $1/4$ cup of this mixture in place of the $1\frac{1}{2}$ tablespoons of commercial caramel color powder in our Pumpernickel Bread (decrease the water in your initial mix by $1/4$ cup).

---

6. **Preheat a baking stone near the middle of the oven to 400°F (20 to 30 minutes),** with an empty metal broiler tray on any rack that won't interfere with the rising bread.

---

7. Using a pastry brush, paint the top crust with cornstarch wash or water and sprinkle with the caraway seeds (if using). Slash the loaf with ½-inch-deep parallel cuts, using a serrated bread knife (see photos, page 71).

8. Slide the loaf directly onto the hot stone. Pour 1 cup of hot water into the broiler tray and quickly close the oven door (see page 28 for steam alternatives). Bake for 35 to 40 minutes, or until firm. (Smaller or larger loaves will require adjustments in baking time.)

9. Allow to cool on a rack before slicing and eating.

VARIATION:
BLACK-AND-WHITE BRAIDED PUMPERNICKEL AND RYE LOAF
Start with ½ pound each of pumpernickel dough and rye dough (pages 125 and 122). Make two long dough-ropes from the rye dough and one thicker rope from the pumpernickel—all three should be the same length. Line up the three ropes, keeping the pumpernickel in the center, and braid them (see the Challah recipe, page 187, if you haven't braided bread dough before). Allow for a 90-minute rest on a prepared pizza peel, then bake at 450°F, with steam, for 35 to 45 minutes, depending on the thickness of the loaf. Allow to cool on a rack before slicing (see color photo).

Pumpernickel Date-and-Walnut Bread

The sweetness of the dried fruit and the richness of the nuts are wonderful with the aromatic pumpernickel dough. We finish the loaf with nothing but the traditional cornstarch wash, letting the fruit and nuts take center stage.

Makes 1 loaf

1 pound (grapefruit-size portion) Pumpernickel Bread dough (page 125)
¼ cup chopped walnuts
¼ cup chopped dates or raisins
Cornmeal or parchment paper, for the pizza peel
Cornstarch wash (see sidebar, page 121) or water, for brushing the loaf

1. Using wet hands instead of flour, cut off a 1-pound (grapefruit-size) piece of dough. Continuing with wet hands, quickly shape it into a ball by stretching the surface of the dough around to the bottom on all four sides, rotating the ball a quarter-turn as you go.

2. Flatten the dough with your wet hands to a thickness of ½ inch and sprinkle with the walnuts and dates. Roll up the dough like a jelly roll, to form a log. Crimp the ends shut and tuck them under to form an oval loaf.

3. Place the loaf on a pizza peel prepared with cornmeal or parchment paper and allow to rest for 90 minutes (see sidebar, page 70).

4. **Preheat a baking stone near the middle of the oven to 400°F (20 to 30 minutes),** with an empty metal broiler tray on any rack that won't interfere with the rising bread.

5. Using a pastry brush, paint the top crust with cornstarch wash or water and then slash the loaf with ½-inch-deep parallel cuts, using a serrated bread knife (see photos, page 71).

6. Slide the loaf directly onto the hot stone. Pour 1 cup of hot water into the broiler tray and quickly close the oven door (see page 28 for steam alternatives). Bake for 35 to 40 minutes, or until firm. (Smaller or larger loaves will require adjustments in baking time.)

7. Allow to cool on a rack before slicing and eating.

100% Whole Wheat Sandwich Bread with Milk and Honey

Whole wheat flour has a nutty, slightly bitter flavor, and it caramelizes very easily, yielding a richly browned and flavorful loaf. We've used milk and honey as tenderizers, but the honey's sweetness also serves as a nice counterpoint to whole wheat's bitter notes. Although we've showcased a loaf pan method here, this dough also makes lovely free-form loaves using the baking stone or a heavy baking sheet.

Makes two 1½-pound loaves, with another pound left over for rolls (see page 108). The recipe can be doubled or halved.

Ingredient	Volume (U.S.)	Weight (U.S.)	Weight (Metric)
Lukewarm water (100°F or below)	1½ cups	12 ounces	340 grams
Lukewarm milk	1½ cups	12 ounces	340 grams
Granulated yeast[1]	1 tablespoon	0.35 ounce	10 grams
Kosher salt[1]	1 to 1½ table-spoons	0.6 to 0.9 ounce	17 to 25 grams
Honey	½ cup	6 ounces	170 grams
Oil, plus additional for greasing the pan	5 tablespoons	2¼ ounces	65 grams
Whole wheat flour	6⅔ cups	1 pound, 14 ounces	850 grams

[1]Can adjust to taste (see pages 18 and 20).

1. **Mixing and storing the dough:** Mix the yeast, salt, honey, and oil with the water and milk in a 6-quart bowl or a lidded (not airtight) food container.

2. Mix in the remaining dry ingredients without kneading, using a spoon or a heavy-duty stand mixer (with the paddle/flat beater). If you're not using a machine, you may need to use wet hands to incorporate the last bit of flour.

3. Cover (not airtight) and allow to rest at room temperature until the dough rises and collapses (or flattens on top), approximately 2 hours.

4. The dough can be used immediately after the initial rise, though it is easier to handle when cold. Refrigerate the container of dough and use over the next 5 days. Freeze (airtight) if you're keeping it longer than that.

5. Grease an 8½ × 4½-inch loaf pan with oil (grease heavily if you're not using a nonstick pan). Using wet hands, scoop out a 1½-pound (small cantaloupe–size) handful of dough. This dough is pretty sticky, and often it's easiest to handle with wet hands. Quickly shape it into a ball by stretching the surface of the dough around to the bottom on all four sides, rotating the ball a quarter-turn as you go. Elongate the ball to form an oval loaf.

6. Drop the loaf into the prepared pan.

7. Cover with plastic wrap and allow to rest for 90 minutes.

8. **Preheat the oven to 350°F,** with a rack set in the middle position. Place an empty metal broiler tray on any rack that won't interfere with the

rising bread. A baking stone is not required, and omitting it shortens the preheat.

9. Flour the top of the loaf and slash, using the tip of a serrated bread knife. Pour 1 cup of hot water into the broiler tray and quickly close the oven door (see page 28 for steam alternatives). Bake for 50 to 60 minutes until deeply browned and firm.

10. Remove from the pan and allow to cool completely before slicing; otherwise, you won't get well-cut sandwich slices (see sidebar, page 87, for slicing tips). If the loaf sticks, wait 10 minutes and it will steam itself out of the pan.

American-Style Whole Wheat Sandwich Bread

Here's a classic American-style whole grain sandwich bread—a blend of grains, some sweetener, and butter that makes for a tender and flavorful loaf. Even though this bread is soft-crusted, we bake it with steam to improve the color and appearance.

Makes 2 loaves, slightly less than 2 pounds each. The recipe can be doubled or halved.

Ingredient	Volume (U.S.)	Weight (U.S.)	Weight (Metric)
Lukewarm water (100°F or below)	3 cups	1 pound, 8 ounces	680 grams
Granulated yeast[1]	1 tablespoon	0.35 ounce	10 grams
Kosher salt[1]	1 to 1½ table-spoons	0.6 to 0.9 ounce	17 to 25 grams
Honey	¼ cup	3 ounces	85 grams
Unsalted butter, melted, or oil, plus additional for greasing the pan	¼ cup	2 ounces	55 grams
Rye flour	¼ cup	1 ounce	30 grams
Whole wheat flour	2¾ cups	13½ ounces	380 grams
All-purpose flour	3 cups	15 ounces	425 grams

[1]Can adjust to taste (see pages 18 and 20).

1. **Mixing and storing the dough:** Mix the yeast, salt, honey, and butter or oil with the water in a 6-quart bowl or a lidded (not airtight) food container.

2. Mix in the remaining dry ingredients without kneading, using a spoon or a heavy-duty stand mixer (with the paddle/flat beater). If you're not using a machine, you may need to use wet hands to incorporate the last bit of flour.

3. Cover (not airtight) and allow to rest at room temperature until the dough rises and collapses (or flattens on top), approximately 2 hours.

4. The dough can be used immediately after the initial rise, though it is easier to handle when cold. Refrigerate the container of dough and use over the next 5 days.

5. Grease an 8½ × 4½-inch loaf pan with oil (grease heavily if you're not using a nonstick pan). Dust the surface of the refrigerated dough with flour and cut off a 1½-pound (small cantaloupe–size) piece. Dust with more flour and quickly shape it into a ball by stretching the surface of the dough around to the bottom on all four sides, rotating the ball a quarter-turn as you go. Elongate to form an oval loaf and place it in the prepared pan. Cover with plastic wrap and allow to rest for 90 minutes (see sidebar, page 70).

6. **Preheat the oven to 400°F,** with a rack set in the middle position. Place an empty metal broiler tray on any rack that won't interfere with the rising bread. A baking stone is not required, and omitting it shortens the preheat.

7. Flour the top of the loaf and slash, using the tip of a serrated bread knife. Pour 1 cup of hot water into the broiler tray and quickly close

the oven door (see page 28 for steam alternatives). Bake for 50 to 55 minutes, or until richly browned and firm. (Smaller or larger loaves will require adjustments in resting and baking time.)

8. Remove from the pan; if it sticks, allow the loaf to rest in the pan for 10 minutes and it will "steam" itself free, then work a spatula around the loaf to nudge it out of the pan. Allow to cool completely before slicing; otherwise, you won't get well-cut sandwich slices (see sidebar, page 87, for slicing tips).

Vermont Cheddar Bread

Great cheese bread is a wonderful American specialty, and a complete meal in a slice. The success of this loaf will depend on the cheese you use, so go with a great one.

"I grew up in Vermont, where eating sharp, aged cheddar is a birthright. Every Vermont bakery offers its own version of cheddar bread, using cheese from local dairies. We lived near Shelburne Farms, and I'm still loyal to their cheddar even since moving to the Midwest. It can be found at Whole Foods and other grocers with a good cheese counter. Feel free to substitute your favorite cheddar or other sharp-flavored hard cheese." —Zoë

Makes four loaves, slightly less than 1 pound each. Recipe can be doubled or halved.

Ingredient	Volume (U.S.)	Weight (U.S.)	Weight (Metric)
Lukewarm water (100°F or below)	3 cups	1 pound, 8 ounces	680 grams
Granulated yeast[1]	1 tablespoon	0.35 ounce	10 grams
Kosher salt[1]	1 to 1½ tablespoons	0.6 to 0.9 ounce	17 to 25 grams
Sugar	1½ tablespoons	¾ ounce	20 grams
All-purpose flour	6½ cups	2 pounds	910 grams
Grated cheddar cheese	1 cup	4 ounces	115 grams
Cornmeal or parchment paper, for the pizza peel			

[1]Can adjust to taste (see pages 18 and 20).

1. **Mixing and storing the dough:** Mix the yeast, salt, and sugar with the water in a 6-quart bowl or a lidded (not airtight) food container.

2. Mix in the dry ingredients and the cheese without kneading, using a spoon or a heavy-duty stand mixer (with the paddle/flat beater). If you're not using a machine, you may need to use wet hands to incorporate the last bit of flour.

3. Cover (not airtight) and allow to rest at room temperature until the dough rises and collapses (or flattens on top), approximately 2 hours.

4. The dough can be used immediately after the initial rise, though it is easier to handle when cold. Refrigerate the container of dough and use over the next 7 days.

5. Dust the surface of the refrigerated dough with flour and cut off a 1-pound (grapefruit-size) piece. Dust the piece with more flour and quickly shape it into a ball by stretching the surface of the dough around to the bottom on all four sides, rotating the ball a quarter-turn as you go. Allow to rest for 1 hour on a pizza peel that has been covered with cornmeal or parchment paper.

6. **Preheat a baking stone near the middle of the oven to 450°F (20 to 30 minutes),** with an empty metal broiler tray on any rack that won't interfere with the rising bread.

7. Sprinkle liberally with flour and slash the top about ½ inch deep, using a serrated bread knife.

8. Slide the loaf directly onto the hot stone. Pour 1 cup of hot water into the broiler tray and quickly close the oven door (see page 28 for steam alternatives). Bake for about 30 minutes, or until richly browned and

firm. (Smaller or larger loaves will require adjustments in resting and baking time.)

9. Allow to cool on a rack before slicing and eating.

VARIATION: CRISP CHEESY BREAD STICKS

To make thin, crispy (and cheesy) bread sticks, follow the directions below with Vermont Cheddar Bread dough. You can also make these with Master, Basic, or European Peasant dough (pages 63–84, or 117)—see color photo.

1. **Preheat the oven to 400°F.** Grease a baking sheet with oil or butter or line with parchment paper. Using a rolling pin, roll the dough out to a ⅛-inch-thick rectangle, about 8 × 13 inches. As you roll the dough, use just enough flour to prevent it from sticking to the work surface. Cut along the long side into ⅛-inch-wide strips, using a pizza cutter or sharp knife.

2. Lay the strips on the prepared baking sheet, spacing them about ½ inch apart. Using a pastry brush, daub olive oil over each strip and sprinkle with coarse salt.

3. Bake the bread sticks in the center of the oven for 10 to 16 minutes. The bread sticks are done when nicely browned and beginning to crisp; they will firm up when cool.

Pain au Potiron (Peppery Pumpkin and Olive Oil Loaf)

Indigenous people were the first Americans to cultivate pumpkin, so it's generally thought of as a quintessentially American ingredient. But there's also a marvelous French Provençal tradition of bread spiked with peppered pumpkin. You can substitute raw winter squash or sweet potato for the pumpkin. Whatever you use, be sure to dice the vegetable small (¼-inch pieces) so that it fully cooks during the baking time (see color photo).

Makes enough dough for four 1-pound loaves. The recipe can be doubled or halved.

Ingredient	Volume (U.S.)	Weight (U.S.)	Weight (Metric)
Whole wheat flour	3¾ cups	17 ounces	485 grams
All-purpose flour	3½ cups	1 pound, 1½ ounces	495 grams
Granulated yeast[1]	1 tablespoon	0.35 ounce	10 grams
Kosher salt[1]	1 to 1½ tablespoons	0.6 to 0.9 ounce	17 to 25 grams
Vital wheat gluten (see page 13)	¼ cup	1⅜ ounces	40 grams
1¼ cups peeled, ¼-inch-dice raw pie pumpkin (sometimes called "sugar" pumpkin), or substitute squash or sweet potato			
Freshly ground black pepper			
Lukewarm water	3½ cups	1 pound, 12 ounces	795 grams
Olive oil	¼ cup	2 ounces	55 grams
Cornmeal or parchment paper, for the pizza peel			

[1]Can adjust to taste (see pages 18 and 20).

1. **Mixing and storing the dough:** Whisk together the flours, yeast, salt, and vital wheat gluten in a 6-quart bowl, or a lidded (not airtight) food container.

2. Generously season the pumpkin, squash, or sweet potato to taste with the pepper.

3. Add the liquid ingredients and pumpkin to the dry ingredients and mix without kneading, using a spoon, or a heavy-duty stand mixer (with the paddle/flat beater). You might need to use wet hands to get the last bit of flour to incorporate if you're not using a machine.

4. Cover (not airtight), and allow the dough to rest at room temperature until it rises and collapses (or flattens on top), approximately 2 hours.

5. The dough can be used immediately after its initial rise, though it is easier to handle when cold. Refrigerate it and use over the next 10 days. The flavor will be best if you wait for at least 24 hours of refrigeration.

6. Dust the surface of the refrigerated dough with flour and cut off a 1-pound (grapefruit-size) piece. Dust with more flour and quickly shape it into a ball by stretching the surface of the dough around to the bottom, rotating the ball a quarter-turn as you go.

7. Elongate the ball into a narrow oval. Place the loaf on a pizza peel prepared with cornmeal or lined with parchment paper, cover loosely with plastic wrap or an overturned bowl, and allow to rest for 90 minutes (40 minutes if you're using fresh, unrefrigerated dough). Alternatively, you can rest the loaf on a silicone mat or a greased baking sheet without using a pizza peel.

8. **Preheat a baking stone near the middle of the oven to 450°F (20 to 30 minutes),** with an empty metal broiler tray on any other rack that won't interfere with the rising bread.

9. Just before baking, use a pastry brush to paint the top crust with water. Slash the loaf diagonally with ½-inch-deep parallel cuts, using a serrated bread knife (see photos, page 71).

10. Slide the loaf directly onto the hot stone (or place the silicone mat or baking sheet on the stone if you used one). Pour 1 cup of hot water into the broiler tray and quickly close the oven door (see page 28 for steam alternatives). Bake for about 35 minutes, or until richly browned and firm. (Smaller or larger loaves will require adjustments in resting and baking time.)

11. Allow the bread to cool on a rack before slicing.

Buttermilk Cinnamon-Raisin Bread

Many traditional American and British breads use buttermilk, which tenderizes the bread, creating a lovely soft crust and crumb and a terrific flavor. With or without the raisins, it's delicious. You can also use this dough, with or without cinnamon and raisins, in any of the classic shapes in Chapter 7, lowering the baking temperature to 375°F and increasing the baking time.

"My friend Judy is the CEO of a successful company. At one tense meeting with her board of directors, she used the simple magic of shaping loaves to win over the skeptics. She slammed the dough onto the conference table. 'Growing a company,' Judy told them, 'is like baking bread. Sometimes you have to be patient and wait for the dough to rise. Things need to develop spontaneously.' She shaped a loaf until a cinnamon-raisin bread was formed, and the board gave its blessing to her company's next stage. She's continued to serve this bread, with butter and jam, at business meetings, tense or otherwise." —Jeff

Makes two loaves, slightly less than 2 pounds each. Recipe can be doubled or halved.

Ingredient	Volume (U.S.)	Weight (U.S.)	Weight (Metric)
Lukewarm water (100°F or below)	2 cups	16 ounces	455 grams
Buttermilk	1 cup	8$\frac{1}{2}$ ounces	240 grams
Granulated yeast[1]	1 tablespoon	0.35 ounce	10 grams
Kosher salt[1]	1 to 1$\frac{1}{2}$ tablespoons	0.6 to 0.9 ounce	17 to 25 grams
Sugar	$\frac{1}{3}$ cup	2$\frac{1}{4}$ ounces	65 grams
Raisins	1$\frac{1}{2}$ cups	7 ounces	200 grams

Visit BreadIn5.com, where you'll find recipes, photos, videos, and instructional material.

Ground cinnamon	1 tablespoon		
All-purpose flour	6½ cups	2 pounds	910 grams
Unsalted butter, melted, or oil for greasing the pan			
Egg wash (see sidebar, page 189), for brushing the loaf			

[1]Can adjust to taste (see pages 18 and 20).

1. **Mixing and storing the dough:** Mix the yeast, salt, sugar, raisins, and cinnamon with the water and buttermilk in a 6-quart bowl or a lidded (not airtight) food container.

2. Mix in the flour without kneading, using a spoon or a heavy-duty stand mixer (with the paddle/flat beater). If you're not using a machine, you may need to use wet hands to incorporate the last bit of flour.

3. Cover (not airtight) and allow to rest at room temperature until the dough rises and collapses (or flattens on top), approximately 2 hours.

4. The dough can be used immediately after the initial rise, though it is easier to handle when cold. Refrigerate the container of dough and use over the next 5 days, or freeze for up to 3 weeks.

5. Grease an 8½ × 4½-inch loaf pan with oil (grease heavily if you're not using a nonstick pan).

6. Dust the surface of the refrigerated dough with flour and cut off a 2-pound (large cantaloupe–size) piece. Dust the piece with more flour and quickly shape it into a ball by stretching the surface of the dough around to the bottom on all four sides, rotating the ball a quarter-turn as you go. Elongate the ball into an oval.

7. Drop the dough into the prepared pan and allow the dough to rest for 90 minutes, loosely covered with plastic wrap.

8. **Preheat the oven to 375°F** and position a rack in the center. A baking stone is not required, and omitting it shortens the preheat.

9. Just before baking, use a pastry brush to brush the top of the loaf with egg wash. Bake the bread for about 50 minutes, or until golden brown.

10. Remove the bread from the pan. Allow to cool completely before slicing (see sidebar, page 87, for slicing tips).

Bagels

Traditional bagels, which come from Eastern Europe, get their texture and flavor from a brief trip into a malty boiling pot before baking (see color photo). You can substitute sugar for the malt in both the dough and the boiling water, but the flavor won't be quite as authentic. Bagels are meant to be chewy, so we use "strong" dough made with bread flour (page 77). But that's not an absolute requirement, and you can use any of the doughs in Chapter 5 or 6 (pages 63–84). If you really want to save time and simplify, try the non-boiled variation (page 148).

Makes 5 bagels

The Bagels
  1 pound (grapefruit-size portion) Strong White Dough with optional malt
    included (page 77)
  Flour, for dusting
  Poppy or sesame seeds, for sprinkling

The Boiling Pot
  8 quarts water
  ¼ cup malt powder, sugar, or honey
  1 teaspoon baking soda

1. **Preheat a baking stone near the middle of the oven to 500°F (20 to 30 minutes),** with an empty metal broiler tray on any rack that won't interfere with the bagels.

2. **Form the bagels:** Dust the surface of the refrigerated dough with flour and cut off a 1-pound (grapefruit-size) piece. Divide the dough into 5 equal pieces. Dust each piece with more flour and quickly shape it into

a ball by stretching the surface of the dough around to the bottom on all four sides, rotating the ball a quarter-turn as you go. Repeat to form the rest of the bagels.

> ∾
>
> **Another way to shape bagels:** Some readers find it easier to pull the dough ball into a thin rope and squeeze the ends together to form the ring.

3. Cover the balls loosely with plastic wrap and allow to rest for 20 minutes.

4. **Prepare the boiling pot:** Put the water in a stockpot and bring to a boil. Reduce to a simmer and add the malt powder, sugar, or honey, and baking soda.

5. Punch your thumb through each dough ball to form a hole. Ease the hole open with your fingers and stretch until the diameter is about triple the width of the bagel wall.

6. Drop the bagels into the simmering water one at a time, raising the flame as necessary to continue at a slow simmer. They need enough room to float without crowding or they will be misshapen (though they may touch a little). Let them simmer for 1 minute and then flip them over with a slotted spoon to cook the other side for another 30 seconds.

7. Remove them from the water using the slotted spoon and place on a clean kitchen towel that has been dusted with flour; this will absorb

A simpler way to bake the boiled bagels: You can skip the traditional floured-towel routine by using the slotted spoon to drop the bagels right onto a heavy-duty baking sheet prepared with a silicone pad or parchment paper. The bagels won't stick to parchment even though they're wet and starchy. Spill or brush off any accumulated water from the parchment, then sprinkle with seeds and bake with steam. You don't need the stone unless you're using it to even out the oven heat.

some of the excess water. After they've drained a bit, place them on a peel covered with whole wheat flour. Sprinkle the bagels with poppy seeds or sesame seeds.

8. Slide the bagels directly onto the hot stone. Pour 1 cup of hot water into the broiler tray and quickly close the oven door (see page 28 for steam alternatives). Bake for 15 to 20 minutes, or until deeply browned and firm.

9. Break the usual rule for cooling and serve these a bit warm.

VARIATION: NON-BOILED ONION-POPPY SEED BAGELS

"Truth be told, I almost never boil bagels anymore. Since I want them fresh every Sunday, I've stopped worrying quite so much about authenticity. There's no question that the texture is different, but when you're using strong-flavored toppings like dried onion flakes, those dominate the overall effect anyway. And don't try to make onion bagels with sautéed onions, as I regrettably once did—nothing says 'New York bagel' like dried onion flakes." —Jeff

After shaping the bagels, skip the boiling bath and drop them onto a heavy-duty baking sheet prepared with parchment paper or a silicone pad. Rest for 20 minutes, brush with water, and sprinkle with dried onion flakes and poppy seeds. If water has collected in the bagel-hole, tilt the pan, loop your finger under the downhill side of the bagel, and allow water to drain to the end of the pan, where you can brush it out. **Bagels topped with dried onion flakes need to be baked at a lower temperature or the flakes will scorch or burn: 400°F for about 25 minutes.**

Soft Pretzels

Pretzels, which originated in Germany, are closely related to bagels, and you can make fantastic ones using our Strong White Dough (page 77), and twisting it into the pretzel shape—an ancient symbol of earth and sun (see color photo). A brief bath in a boiling alkaline solution (we use baking soda) transforms ordinary bread crust into the essence of pretzels. We love them warm, with mustard.

"Food writer Mimi Sheraton wrote a newspaper article on homemade pretzels about forty years ago, and it stuck in my teenage mind—I was taken by her description of the crusty pretzels baked by her Stuttgart hosts. I still have the original clipping from 1978, so we've adapted her recipe here." —Jeff

Makes 5 pretzels

The Pretzels
  1 pound (grapefruit-size portion) Strong White Dough (page 77)
  Flour, for dusting
  Coarse salt (or "pretzel" salt, which can be found in specialty shops)
  Whole wheat flour, for the pizza peel

The Boiling Pot
  8 quarts water
  ¼ cup baking soda
  2 tablespoons sugar

1. **Form the pretzels:** Dust the surface of the refrigerated dough with flour and cut off a 1-pound (grapefruit-size) piece. Divide the dough into 5 equal pieces. Dust each piece with more flour and quickly shape it into a ball by stretching the surface of the dough around to the bottom on all four sides, rotating the ball a quarter-turn as you go.

Elongate the ball, dusting with additional flour as necessary. Roll it back and forth with your hands on a flour-dusted surface to form a long rope about 20 inches long, approximately ½ inch in diameter at the center, and tapered on the ends.

2. Twist the dough rope into a pretzel shape by first forming a horseshoe with the ends facing away from you. Fold the tapered ends down to the thick part of the rope, crossing them, one over the other. Extend the ends an inch beyond the bottom loop and gently press them together.

3. **Preheat a baking stone near the middle of the oven to 450°F (20 to 30 minutes),** with an empty metal broiler tray on any rack that won't interfere with the rising pretzels.

4. Keep the pretzels covered loosely with plastic wrap as you repeat the process to shape the remaining dough. Let the pretzels rest at room temperature for 20 minutes.

5. **Prepare the boiling pot:** Put the water in a stockpot and bring to a boil. Reduce to a simmer and add the baking soda and sugar. Drop the pretzels into the simmering water one at a time, making sure they are not crowding one another. They need enough room to float without touching or they will be misshapen. Let them simmer for 1 minute and then flip them over with a slotted spoon to cook the other side for another 30 seconds.

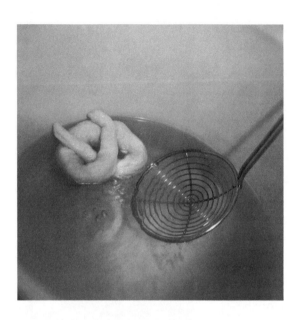

6. Remove them from the water using the slotted spoon and place on a clean kitchen towel that has been dusted with flour. This will absorb some of the excess water from the pretzels. Then place them on a peel covered with whole wheat flour. Sprinkle with coarse salt.

7. Slide the pretzels directly onto the hot stone. Pour 1 cup of hot water into the broiler tray and quickly close the oven

We didn't use lye in the boiling pot: When we published a pretzel recipe in an earlier book, a few people wrote to express their dismay that we didn't use lye in the boiling pot—that's right, the same alkaline chemical used in drain cleaner. They claimed that it's the crucial ingredient to get the absolutely authentic German-style pretzel crust they craved. They may have a point, but we doubted we'd be able to convince home bakers to try this particularly wacky ingredient. We actually went so far as to purchase food-grade lye, but then we read the label: "... *wear chemical-resistant gloves. Wear protective clothing. Wear goggles...*" And our favorite, advising users to watch out for *"digestive tract burns"* (though the manufacturer helpfully advises against swallowing the lye). We found that baking soda makes a terrific substitute—it's alkaline enough. We must admit, we never opened that container of lye.

door (see page 28 for steam alternatives). Bake for about 15 minutes, or until deeply browned and firm. If you want crisp pretzels, bake 5 to 10 minutes longer.

8. Serve these a bit warm, with a hefty stein of beer.

VARIATION: PRETZEL BUNS

Divide a 1-pound ball of Strong White Dough (page 77) into 8 smooth balls; allow to rest for 20 minutes. Boil as in the main recipe, but **shorten the boil to 20 seconds on each side,** drain, and space 2 inches apart on a baking sheet prepared with oil, butter, parchment paper, or a silicone mat. Sprinkle with coarse salt and bake with steam for 20 minutes at 450°F.

Yeasted Thanksgiving Cornbread with Cranberries

Traditional American cornbread is a butter- or lard-enriched quick bread, risen with baking powder and baking soda. We make ours with a yeasted, corn-enriched dough. For Thanksgiving, we studded the dough with sweetened cranberries. Playing on the American cornbread theme, we baked the loaf in a heated cast-iron pan, liberally greased with butter, lard, bacon grease, or oil, which created a rich and flavorful crust. Like a baking stone, cast iron absorbs and retains heat well, and radiates it very evenly to the dough, promoting a nice brown crust (see color photo).

Makes 3 loaves

Ingredient	Volume (U.S.)	Weight (U.S.)	Weight (Metric)
Lukewarm water (100°F or below)	3 cups	1 pound, 8 ounces	680 grams
Granulated yeast[1]	1 tablespoon	0.35 ounce	10 grams
Kosher salt[1]	1 to 1½ tablespoons	0.6 to 0.9 ounce	17 to 25 grams
Sugar	⅔ cup	4½ ounces	130 grams
Cornmeal	1½ cups	8½ ounces	240 grams
All-purpose flour	5 cups	1 pound, 9 ounces	710 grams
1 cup (4 ounces/115 grams) fresh cranberries or ⅓ cup dried (1½ ounces/45 grams)			
Zest of 1 orange, grated with a microplane zester (see page 38), avoid the white pith			
Unsalted butter, lard, bacon grease, or oil, for greasing the pan			

[1]Can adjust to taste (see pages 18 and 20).

1. **Mixing and storing the dough:** Mix the dough as in the Master Recipe (page 63), incorporating the sugar, cranberries, and orange zest with the water. Rise, rest, and store the dough for use as needed for up to 7 days in the refrigerator.

2. Dust the surface of the refrigerated dough with flour and cut off a 1½-pound (small cantaloupe–size) piece. Dust the piece with more flour and quickly shape it into a ball by stretching the surface of the dough around to the bottom on all four sides, rotating the ball a quarter-turn as you go.

3. Grease a cast-iron pan with the butter, lard, bacon grease, or oil, being sure to coat the sides of the pan as well. Place the dough in the pan. Cover with plastic wrap or the pan's lid and allow the dough to rest for 90 minutes.

4. **Preheat the oven to 425°F,** with an empty metal broiler tray on any rack that won't interfere with the rising bread. A baking stone is not required, and omitting it shortens the preheat.

5. Just before baking, uncover and heat the pan over medium heat for 1 or 2 minutes to jump-start the baking process and promote caramelization of the bottom crust.

6. Place the pan on a rack near the center of the oven. Pour 1 cup of hot water into the broiler tray and quickly close the oven door (see page 28 for steam alternatives). Check for browning in 20 minutes. The time required will depend on the size and weight of the pan, but will probably be 30 minutes. The loaf should be a rich yellow-brown when done.

7. Carefully turn the hot loaf out of the pan onto a serving plate, or just cut wedges directly from the pan.

9

PIZZA AND FLATBREADS

Flatbreads from southern Europe, like Italian *focaccia* and French Provençal *fougasse*, have been popular in the United States for years (though not as long as pizza). When they first arrived on the scene, they seemed rich and exotic, with their strong flavors and their dependence on luxurious, savory olive oil. But their originators would have laughed—this was simple peasant fare, without pretension. These fragrant rounds were born in regions where dairy and butter were greater luxuries than olive oil.

Once they've had their brief rest, flatbreads also bake very quickly, so if you've stored some dough, you can have fresh flatbread on the table in about twenty-five minutes.

Pizza Margherita: A Classic, with Mozzarella, Tomato, and Basil (but top however you like!)

We like crisp, thin-crusted, Neapolitan (Naples) style pizza, baked at a high temperature directly on the stone. In home ovens, the maximum temperature is 500°F or 550°F, not 905°F as in Naples, but baking right on a stone helps achieve a crisp crust even at the lower temperature. Pizza made this way at home, especially if you can get fresh mozzarella, is unlike anything most of us are used to eating (almost as good: you can also bake pizza on a greased heavy-duty baking sheet). The secret to Neapolitan pizza is to keep the crust thin, avoid watery sauces or toppings, don't overload it, and bake it very quickly at a high temperature so it doesn't all cook down to a soup— you should be able to appreciate the individual ingredients in the topping. Use any toppings you like on this pizza—sautéed mushrooms or other vegetables, browned sausage slices, pepperoni . . . the list goes on. Preparing the crust is very much like preparing dough for pita (see page 100), so consider starting with that recipe before you tackle pizza.

Makes one 12-inch pizza; serves 2 to 4

½ pound/225 grams (orange-size piece), any Master, Basic, or European Peasant dough (pages 63–84, or 117)

⅓ cup (3 ounces/85 grams) tomato topping (see sidebar)

3 ounces (85 grams) fresh mozzarella cheese, cut into ½-inch chunks

6 fresh basil leaves, thinly slivered or torn

Flour, cornmeal, or parchment paper for the pizza peel

1. **Preheat a baking stone to your oven's highest temperature (550°F or 500°F),** placing the stone near the bottom of the oven to help crisp the bottom crust without burning the cheese. Most stones will be hot

enough in 40 minutes (see page 54 for longer preheat options). You won't be using steam, so omit the broiler tray.

2. Prepare and measure all the toppings in advance. The key to a pizza that slides right off the peel is to work quickly—don't let the dough sit on the peel any longer than necessary.

3. Prepare a pizza peel with flour, cornmeal, or parchment paper.

4. Dust the surface of the refrigerated dough with flour and cut off a ½-pound (orange-size) piece. Dust the piece with more flour and

Tomato toppings:

*   **Cooked pizza sauce:** A perfectly smooth, thick pizza sauce is easier to work with, especially when you're starting out, because it's easier to apply thinly. That's important with high-moisture dough, since excess liquid can cause a soggy crust. Start with canned tomatoes (whole, diced, crushed, or pureed) and process them in a food processor until smooth. Then simmer in a saucepan over medium-low heat until thickened. Or make a thick, slightly sweet sauce by processing one 6-ounce can tomato paste with one 14½-ounce can of diced tomatoes. This makes enough sauce for several pizzas and doesn't require draining or reduction of liquid to produce a thick, pizza-ready sauce (save the liquid for something else).

*   **Uncooked tomato topping:** Use canned or fresh tomatoes without reducing or heating them by crushing them and then placing them in a strainer and pressing out as much liquid as you can.

*   **Flavoring the topping:** Add any of these to your sauce reduction or uncooked tomatoes: garlic, sautéed onion, oregano, basil, capers, anchovies. Be creative!

quickly shape it into a ball by stretching the surface of the dough around to the bottom on all four sides, rotating the ball a quarter-turn as you go. If you have time, drape with plastic wrap and allow to rest for up to 60 minutes (this will make it easier to achieve a thin crust).

5. Prepare a pizza peel with flour, cornmeal, or parchment paper. As you get better at sliding your pies off the peel, you can use less flour or cornmeal, but be generous while you're learning.

6. Flatten the dough with your hands and a rolling pin on the work surface to produce a $\frac{1}{8}$-inch-thick round and dust with flour to keep the dough from sticking. A little sticking can be helpful in overcoming the dough's resistance to stretch, so don't overuse flour, and consider using a dough scraper to "unstick" the dough. You may also need to let the partially rolled dough sit for a few minutes to "relax" to allow further rolling. At this point, stretching by hand may help, followed by additional rolling. Place the rolled-out dough on the prepared pizza peel. (If you're squeamish about sliding topped pizzas into the oven, consider "baking blind" before topping, in the variations below.)

7. Spread tomato topping over the surface of the dough with a spoon (smooth sauces apply well with a pastry brush). Do not cover the dough thickly or your crust will not crisp.

8. Scatter the mozzarella over the surface of the dough. No further resting is needed prior to baking.

9. If you have an exhaust fan, turn it on now, because some of the flour on the pizza peel will smoke at this temperature (see sidebar). Place the tip of the peel near the back of the stone, close to where you want the far edge of the pizza to land. Give the peel a few quick forward-and-back jiggles and pull it sharply toward you, out from under the

pizza. Check for doneness in 8 to 10 minutes; at this time, turn the pizza around in the oven if one side is browning faster than the other. It may need 5 or more minutes in the oven, depending on your pizza's thickness and your oven's temperature.

10. Remove from the oven with a pizza peel, place on a cooling rack, and scatter with the basil. Allow to cool slightly on a cooling rack before serving to allow the cheese to set.

∞

Don't get smoked out of house and home: An exhaust fan helps because there may be smoke with such a hot stone, especially if you're using cornmeal and have been liberal with it. Make sure the stone is scraped clean before preheating. If you don't have an exhaust fan and smoke is a problem, choose a lower oven temperature (450°F) and bake for 15 to 20 percent longer.

PIZZA VARIATIONS

Thicker-crusted American-style pizza: Use twice as much dough and stretch/roll the crust to a thickness of ¼ inch, which will support a thicker layer of toppings. Oven temperature remains the same, but baking time may be longer. For a really thick "Sicilian-style" pizza, use four times as much dough, stretch to ½ inch thick, and bake on a greased rimmed heavy-duty baking sheet.

Thin cracker-crust: Use half as much dough (¼ pound/peach-size) and roll it out very thinly, to about 1/16 inch. Use half the toppings so that the crust isn't weighed down and grate the cheese rather than using chunks. There's more on cracker-crust, with photos, at BreadIn5.com/CrackerCrustPizza.

Baking "blind": If you really want a crisp crust, or if you like lots of toppings and you're getting sogginess, consider baking the crust "blind." Puncture the rolled-out dough all over with the times of a fork and bake *without toppings* for about 5 minutes. If the crust starts puffing, poke it with a long-handled barbecue fork to deflate. When the crust is just beginning to brown, remove from the oven, add toppings, and complete the baking. When making multiple pizzas for a crowd, this is much more practical than struggling with unbaked dough-rounds.

Pizza or pita on the gas grill: You can try this on a charcoal- or wood-fired grill, but it's much less reliable and takes a lot more practice. Even on a gas grill, you'll need to practice a bit to get the toppings to heat through without burning the crust. Bring your prepared dough round and all ingredients to your preheated outdoor grill.

1. **Preheat** a gas grill with medium flame on all burners.

2. **Direct heat: Bake the crust "blind," without toppings** by sliding the dough onto the grate, directly over the lit burners, and close the lid. After 2 to 3 minutes (depending on your grill), flip the dough with a spatula. The underside should be browned, and the top surface should be puffy (puncture with a fork if it's puffing too much).

3. **Use indirect and direct heat:** Once you flip the pizza, you'll use a combination of indirect and direct heat (avoiding the lit burners, or baking directly over them) to finish baking without burning the crust. In some grills, you can shut off part of the burner element to create a cool spot, which can be very helpful. **Top the pizza** (or not, if you're making pita bread), use mostly indirect heat, and close the lid. Keep an eye on it and use your nose to detect any scorching, moving the pizza around the grill to fully heat the toppings and melt the cheese before the bottom crust burns.

Focaccia with Onion and Rosemary

This is the classic Tuscan hors d'oeuvre: onion and rosemary topping an olive oil–dough flatbread. Try it with something simple, like rustic antipasto, or as an accompaniment to soups or pastas. Bake it on a rimmed baking sheet rather than directly on a stone since the oil would leak onto the stone and create an annoying problem with kitchen smoke that would continue into your next several baking sessions.

The key to success with this recipe is to go light on the onion. If you completely cover the dough surface with onions, the focaccia won't brown and the result, though delicious, will be pale.

Makes 6 appetizer portions

Olive oil, for greasing the baking sheet

1 pound (grapefruit-size portion) Olive Oil Dough (our first choice, page 75), or any Master, Basic, or European Peasant dough (pages 63–84, or 117)

¼ medium white or yellow onion, thinly sliced

2 tablespoons olive oil, preferably extra virgin, plus 1 teaspoon for drizzling

¾ teaspoon dried rosemary leaves (or 1½ teaspoons fresh)

Coarse salt and freshly ground pepper, for sprinkling the top

1. **Preheat a baking stone near the middle of the oven to 425°F (20 to 30 minutes),** with an empty metal broiler tray on any rack that won't interfere with the rising focaccia. The baking stone is not essential when using a baking sheet; if you omit the stone, the preheat can be as short as 5 minutes.

2. Grease a rimmed baking sheet with olive oil or line with parchment paper or a silicone mat. Set aside. Dust the surface of the refrigerated

dough with flour and cut off a 1-pound (grapefruit-size) piece. Dust the piece with more flour and quickly shape it into a ball by stretching the surface of the dough around to the bottom on all four sides, rotating the ball a quarter-turn as you go.

3. Flatten it into a ½- to ¾-inch-thick round, using your hands and/or a rolling pin and a minimal amount of flour. Place the round on the prepared baking sheet.

4. In a skillet, sauté the onion slices over medium heat in 2 tablespoons of the olive oil until softened but not browned; if you brown them they'll burn in the oven. Strew the onion over the surface of the dough, leaving a 1-inch border at the edge. Allow some of the dough surface to show through the onion; you may have some leftover onion at the end. If you can't see much dough surface, you're using too much onion and your focaccia won't brown attractively.

5. Sprinkle with the rosemary and coarse salt, and freshly ground black pepper to taste. Drizzle with the remaining 1 teaspoon olive oil.

6. Allow the focaccia to rest for 20 minutes.

7. After the focaccia has rested, place the baking sheet on a rack in the center of the oven. Pour 1 cup of hot water into the broiler tray and quickly close the oven door (see page 28 for steam alternatives). Bake for about 25 minutes, or until the crust is medium brown. Be careful not to burn the onions. The baking time will vary according to the focaccia's thickness. Focaccia will not develop a crackling crust, because of the olive oil.

8. Cut into wedges and serve warm.

VARIATION: CHERRY–BLACK PEPPER FOCACCIA

Omit the onions and rosemary. While the oven is heating, soak ½ cup (3½ ounces/95 grams) dried cherries in a bowl with ¼ cup red wine, ¼ cup water, ½ teaspoon black pepper, ¼ cup finely minced shallots, and a pinch of salt. Simmer in a saucepan for 5 minutes, then strain. Just before baking, press the cherries into the dough surface so they won't pop off when baking. Drizzle with olive oil, sprinkle with salt and pepper, and bake as above (see color photo).

VARIATION: ONION PLETZEL

Decrease the oven temperature to 350°F, and use Challah (page 187) or Brioche (page 195) dough. Grease the pan with butter or oil, omit the rosemary, and sprinkle the onions with poppy seeds just before baking, approximately 25 minutes (see color photo).

Olive Fougasse

Provençal fougasse and Italian focaccia share a linguistic and culinary background. It's said that both may have ancient Greek or Etruscan roots. Fougasse distinguishes itself with artful cutouts that resemble a leaf or ladder; this delivers a crustier flatbread, with lots more surface exposed to the oven heat. As with focaccia, it's best to bake it on a baking sheet to prevent oil from being absorbed into your baking stone (see color photo).

Makes 6 appetizer portions

1 pound (grapefruit-size portion) Olive Oil Dough (our first choice, page 75), or any Master, Basic, or European Peasant dough (pages 63–84, or 117)

½ cup high-quality black olives, preferably Kalamata or Niçoise, pitted and halved or quartered if large

Olive oil, for greasing the baking sheet and brushing the fougasse

Flour, for dusting the pizza peel

1. **Preheat a baking stone near the middle of the oven to 400°F (20 to 30 minutes),** with an empty metal broiler tray on any rack that won't interfere with the rising bread. Grease a baking sheet with a bit of olive oil. Set aside. The baking stone is not essential for breads made on a baking sheet; if you omit it the preheat can be as short as 5 minutes.

2. Dust the surface of the refrigerated dough with flour and cut off a 1-pound (grapefruit-size) piece. Dust the piece with more flour and quickly shape it into a ball by stretching the surface of the dough around to the bottom on all four sides, rotating the ball a quarter-turn as you go.

3. Flatten the mass of dough to a thickness of about ½ inch on a work surface dusted with flour and sprinkle it with the olives. Roll up the dough, jelly-roll style, then shape it into a ball. Now re-form a flat round approximately ½ inch thick. Place the round on a pizza peel liberally dusted with flour.

4. Cut angled slits into the circle of dough (see photo). You may need to add more flour to be able to cut the slits and keep them spread adequately during baking so they don't close up. Gently pull the holes to open them.

5. Gently lift the slitted dough round onto the prepared baking sheet and brush with additional olive oil. Allow it to rest for 20 minutes.

6. Place the baking sheet with the fougasse near the middle of the oven. Pour 1 cup of hot water into the broiler tray and quickly close the oven door (see page 28 for steam alternatives). Check for doneness at about 20 minutes and continue baking until golden brown, which may be 5 minutes longer. The fougasse will not develop a crackling crust because of the olive oil.

7. Serve warm.

Fougasse Stuffed with Roasted Red Pepper

This is a very festive folded flatbread with a roasted red pepper filling (see color photo). It uses some of the same techniques used in making the olive fougasse, but the dough is folded after slitting, on one side only, to reveal the roasted red pepper layered inside. The rich and smoky red pepper perfumes the whole loaf. It's a fantastic and impressive hors d'oeuvre, sliced or just broken into pieces.

Makes 6 appetizer portions

½ pound (orange-size portion) Olive Oil Dough (our first choice, page 75),
   or any Master, Basic, or European Peasant dough (pages 63–84, or 117)
1 red bell pepper
Coarse salt, for sprinkling
¼ teaspoon dried thyme
Olive oil, preferably extra virgin, for brushing the loaf
Whole wheat flour, for the pizza peel

1. **Preheat a baking stone near the middle of the oven to 450°F (20 to 30 minutes),** with an empty metal broiler tray on any rack that won't interfere with the rising bread.

2. Halve the pepper, removing stem and seeds, and make additional cuts as needed to flatten. Grill or broil the pepper under the broiler or on a gas or charcoal grill, keeping the skin side closest to the heat source. Check often and remove when the skin is blackened, 8 to 10 minutes. Drop the roasted pieces into an empty bowl and cover the bowl. As they steam, the skin will loosen over the next 10 minutes. Gently hand-peel the pepper and discard the blackened skin. Some flavorful dark bits may adhere to the pepper's flesh. Cut the pepper into strips.

3. Dust the surface of the refrigerated dough with flour and cut off a ½-pound (orange-size) piece. Dust the piece with more flour and quickly shape it into a ball by stretching the surface of the dough around to the bottom on all four sides, rotating the ball a quarter-turn as you go.

4. Using a rolling pin, roll the dough out to a large flat oval or rectangle approximately ⅛ inch thick. Add a little more flour than usual when cloaking, shaping, and rolling the dough, because you will need to be able to cut slits into the dough that do not close and immediately re-adhere to one another. Place the dough on a flour-covered pizza peel.

5. Cut angled slits into the dough on only one half of the oval (see the photo below). You may need to add more flour to decrease stickiness so the slits stay open during handling. Gently spread the holes open with your fingers.

6. Place the roasted red pepper strips in a single layer on the unslit side of the fougasse, leaving a 1-inch border at the edge. Sprinkle with coarse salt and thyme. Dampen the dough edge, fold the slitted side over to cover the peppers, and pinch to seal. The peppers should peek brightly through the slitted windows. Brush the loaf with olive oil.

7. Slide the fougasse directly onto the hot stone. Pour 1 cup of hot water

into the broiler tray and quickly close the oven door (see page 28 for steam alternatives). Bake for about 25 minutes, or until golden brown.

8. Allow to cool, then slice or break into pieces and serve.

∾

Jarred roasted red peppers can be swapped for homemade in a pinch. The flavor won't be as intense, but they're a reasonable substitute.

10

GLUTEN-FREE BREADS

Gluten is a protein found in wheat, rye, barley, and in all wheat variants, including spelt, semolina, durum, einkorn, emmer, kamut, bulgur, graham, triticale, freekeh, and farro. People with celiac disease can't eat gluten—doing so causes major health problems. Other medical conditions may make gluten troublesome for others, but there's no evidence to support the idea that everyone should avoid gluten.

For people who don't eat wheat or gluten, we wrote an entire book: ***Gluten-Free Artisan Bread in Five Minutes a Day*** (2014). In that book, we assumed people would be baking gluten-free exclusively, so all its recipes are based on custom flour mixtures, made up in bulk. ***The Best of Artisan Bread in Five Minutes a Day*** assumes that you're a wheat and gluten eater who occasionally needs a gluten-free loaf for a guest, so all of the following recipes are stand-alone—they don't call for pre-mixed flour combinations. We developed our own custom flour ratios through careful testing, because we found commercial mixtures that worked well for cookies and other sweets, but not for breads. Gluten-free bread is persnickety—slight changes in quantity or flour brand make a major difference. We tested with Bob's Red Mill gluten-free flours because they're available all over the United States and give consistent results. If you swap in something else, you'll have to experiment with ratios and water levels.

These doughs are easy to prepare, but they must be handled differently, since there isn't any stretch or structure. A helpful video is on our website at BreadIn5.com/GlutenFreeVideo. **And while you can mix gluten-free dough by hand, we had best results with a stand mixer (page 37).**

Crisp Cheesy Bread Sticks, page 139

Pain au Potiron (Peppery Pumpkin and Olive Oil Loaf), page 140

Bagels, page 146

Soft Pretzels, page 150

Yeasted Thanksgiving Cornbread with Cranberries, page 154

Cherry–Black Pepper Focaccia, page 165

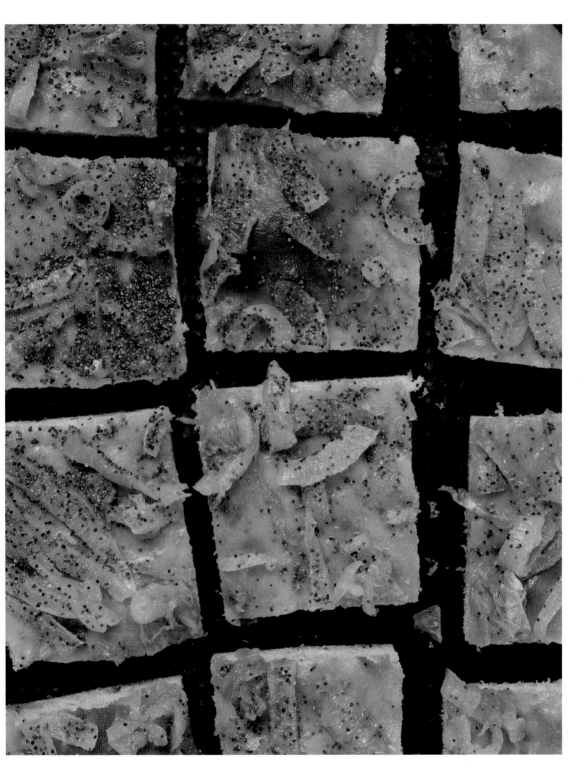

Onion Pletzel, page 165

Gluten-Free Crusty Boule, page 173

Challah, page 187, and Turban-Shaped Challah with Raisins, page 193

Apples and Honey Challah, page 192

Brioche à Tête, page 198

Sticky Caramel Rolls, page 205

Sunny-Side-Up Apricot Pastry, page 211

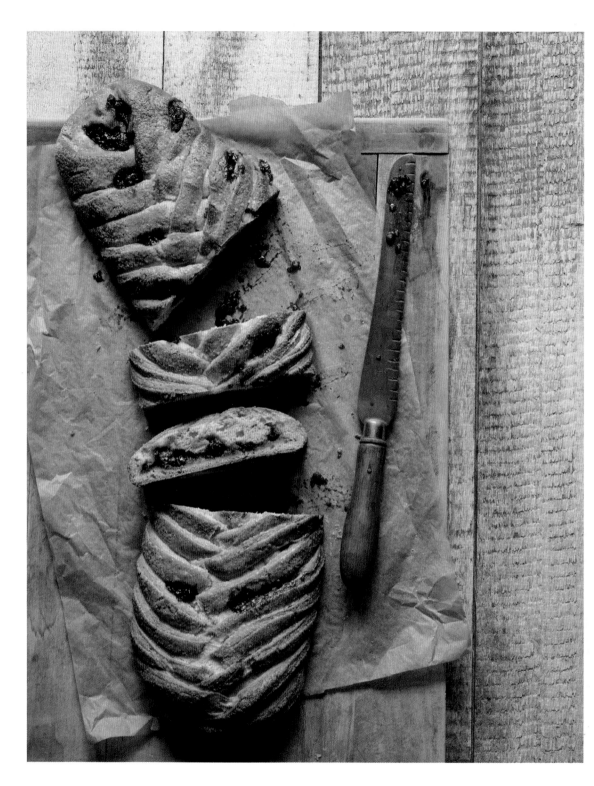

Raspberry Braid, page 219

100% Whole Wheat Christmas Stollen, page 229

Sourdough starter, page 231 (Never tighten a screw-top lid on dough!)

Gluten-Free Crusty Boule

This dough is incredibly versatile; it works beautifully as a classic boule or in a loaf pan for sandwiches (see color photo). It also makes a wonderful pizza crust with your favorite toppings, and it makes great crackers if rolled thin.

Makes enough dough for at least four 1-pound loaves. The recipe can be doubled or halved.

Ingredient	Volume (U.S.)	Weight (U.S.)	Weight (Metric)
Brown rice flour	2 cups	10¾ ounces	305 grams
Sorghum flour	1½ cups	7½ ounces	210 grams
Tapioca flour (tapioca starch)	3 cups	13½ ounces	385 grams
Granulated yeast	2 tablespoons	0.7 ounce	20 grams
Kosher salt[1]	1 tablespoon	0.6 ounce	15 grams
Xanthan gum or ground psyllium husk[2]	2 tablespoons	¾ ounce	20 grams
Lukewarm water	2⅔ cups	1 pound, 5⅓ ounces	605 grams
Large eggs at room temperature, lightly beaten	4	8 ounces	225 grams
Oil (see page 21 for options)	⅓ cup	2½ ounces	70 grams
Honey	2 tablespoons	1½ ounces	45 grams
Cornmeal or parchment paper, for the pizza peel			

[1]Can adjust to taste (see page 20).
[2]Double quantity if using psyllium.

---

1. **Mixing and storing the dough:** Whisk together the flours, yeast, salt, and xanthan gum (or psyllium husk) in a 6-quart bowl or a lidded (not airtight) food container.

2. Combine the liquid ingredients and gradually mix them with the dry ingredients, using a spoon or a heavy-duty stand mixer (with the paddle/flat beater), until all of the dry ingredients are well incorporated. You might have to use wet hands to get the last bit of flour to incorporate if you're not using a machine. *We highly recommend the mixer for gluten-free doughs.*

3. Cover (not airtight), and allow the dough to rest at room temperature until it rises, approximately 2 hours.

4. The dough can be used immediately after the initial rise. Refrigerate in a lidded (not airtight) container and use over the next 7 days; freeze (airtight) if you're keeping it longer than that. The flavor will be best if you wait for at least 24 hours of refrigeration.

5. Use wet hands to take out a 1-pound (grapefruit-size) piece of the refrigerated dough. Quickly shape it into a ball; this dough isn't stretched because there is no gluten in it—just gently press it into the shape. You might need to wet your hands a little to prevent the dough from sticking and to create a smooth surface, but don't use so much water as to make the dough soggy.

6. Place the loaf on a pizza peel prepared with cornmeal or lined with parchment paper, cover loosely with plastic wrap or an overturned bowl, and allow to rest for 90 minutes (40 minutes if you're using fresh, unrefrigerated dough). Alternatively, you can rest the loaf on a silicone mat or a greased baking sheet.

7. **Thirty minutes before baking time, preheat the oven to 450°F, with a baking stone placed on the middle rack.** Place an empty metal broiler tray on any other rack that won't interfere with the rising bread. A baking stone is not required, and omitting it shortens the preheat.

8. Just before baking, slash the loaf with ½-inch-deep parallel cuts, using a serrated bread knife (see photos, page 71).

9. Slide the loaf directly onto the hot stone (or place the silicone mat or baking sheet on the stone if you used one). Pour 1 cup of hot tap water into the broiler tray and quickly close the oven door (see page 28 for steam alternatives). Bake for about 35 minutes, or until lightly browned and firm. If you used parchment paper, a silicone mat, or a baking sheet under the loaf, carefully remove it two-thirds of the way through the baking time and bake the loaf directly on the stone or an oven rack. (Smaller or larger loaves will require adjustments in resting and baking time.)

10. Allow to cool completely on a rack before slicing.

VARIATION: GLUTEN-FREE SANDWICH BREAD
Mix the dough as above, steps 1 through 4.

1. Heavily grease an 8½ × 4½-inch nonstick loaf pan. Use wet hands to break off a 2-pound (cantaloupe–size) piece of the refrigerated dough. Quickly shape it into a ball; this dough isn't stretched be-cause there is no gluten in it—just gently press it into shape. You might need to wet your hands a little more to prevent the dough from sticking and to create a smooth surface, but don't use so much water as to make the dough soggy.

2. Pat the ball into a narrow oval and put it in the loaf pan. Allow the loaf to rest, loosely covered with plastic wrap, for 90 minutes (40 minutes if you're using fresh, unrefrigerated dough).

3. **Thirty minutes before baking time, preheat the oven to 425°F.** Place an empty metal broiler tray on any rack that won't interfere with the rising bread. Just before baking, use a pastry brush to paint the top with water, then sprinkle it with sesame seeds. Place the pan on a rack near the center of the oven.

4. Pour 1 cup of hot tap water into the broiler tray and quickly close the oven door (see page 28 for steam alternatives). Bake for about 55 to 60 minutes, or until richly browned and firm. (Smaller or larger loaves will require adjustments in resting and baking time.)

5. Remove the bread from the pan and allow it to cool on a rack before slicing.

Not Rye, But So Very Close

We both grew up eating rye bread, so when we decided to add gluten-free to our repertoire, we made a list of the essentials, and rye was at the top. In place of rye, which has gluten, we've used teff flour, which is completely gluten-free. It has a sweet-sour molasses flavor that lends itself perfectly to a mock rye bread. With caraway seeds, it's a terrific imposter.

Makes enough dough for at least four 1-pound loaves. The recipe can be doubled or halved.

Ingredient	Volume (U.S.)	Weight (U.S.)	Weight (Metric)
Brown rice flour	2 cups	10^2/$_3$ ounces	305 grams
Teff flour	1^1/$_2$ cups	8 ounces	225 grams
Tapioca flour (tapioca starch)	3 cups	13^1/$_2$ ounces	385 grams
Granulated yeast	2 tablespoons	0.7 ounce	20 grams
Kosher salt[1]	1 tablespoon	0.6 ounce	15 grams
Xanthan gum or ground psyllium husk[2]	2 tablespoons	^{3}/$_4$ ounce	20 grams
Caraway seeds	^{1}/$_4$ cup	1^1/$_4$ ounces	35 grams
Lukewarm water	2^2/$_3$ cups	1 pound, 5^1/$_3$ ounces	605 grams
Large eggs at room temperature, lightly beaten	4	8 ounces	225 grams
Oil (see page 21 for options) or melted unsalted butter	^{1}/$_3$ cup	2^1/$_2$ ounces	70 grams
Honey	2 tablespoons	1^1/$_2$ ounces	45 grams
Molasses	2 tablespoons	1^1/$_4$ ounces	35 grams
Cornmeal or parchment paper, for the pizza peel			

[1]Can adjust to taste (see page 20).
[2]Double quantity if using psyllium.

1. **Mixing and storing the dough:** Whisk together the flours, yeast, salt, xanthan gum, and caraway seeds in a 6-quart bowl or a lidded (not airtight) food container.

2. Combine the liquid ingredients and gradually mix them with the dry ingredients without kneading, using a spoon or a heavy-duty stand mixer (with the paddle/flat beater), until all the dry ingredients are well incorporated. *We highly recommend the mixer for gluten-free doughs.*

3. Cover (not airtight), and allow the dough to rest at room temperature for approximately 2 hours.

4. The dough can be used immediately after its initial rise, or you can refrigerate it in a lidded (not airtight) container and use over the next 7 days; freeze (airtight) if you're keeping it longer than that. The flavor will be best if you wait for at least 24 hours of refrigeration.

5. Use wet hands to take out a 1-pound (grapefruit-size) piece of the refrigerated dough. Quickly shape it into a ball; this dough isn't stretched because there is no gluten in it—just gently press it into the shape. You might need to wet your hands a little more to prevent the dough from sticking and to create a smooth surface, but don't use so much water as to make the dough soggy.

6. Pat the ball into a narrow oval. Place the loaf on a pizza peel prepared with cornmeal or parchment paper, cover loosely with plastic wrap or an overturned bowl, and allow to rest for 90 minutes (40 minutes if you're using fresh, unrefrigerated dough). Alternatively, you can rest the loaf on a silicone mat or a greased baking sheet without using a pizza peel.

7. **Thirty minutes before baking time, preheat the oven to 450°F,** with a
    baking stone placed on the middle rack. Place an empty metal broiler
    tray on any other rack that won't interfere with the rising bread.

8. Just before baking, use a pastry brush to paint the loaf's top crust with
    water and sprinkle it with caraway seeds. Slash the dough with
    ½-inch-deep parallel cuts, using a serrated bread knife (see photos,
    page 71).

9. Slide the loaf directly onto the hot stone (or place the silicone mat or
    baking sheet on the stone if you used one). Pour 1 cup of hot tap water
    into the broiler tray and quickly close the oven door (see page 28 for
    steam alternatives). Bake for about 30 minutes, or until richly browned
    and firm. If you used parchment paper, a silicone mat, or a baking
    sheet under the loaf, carefully remove it two-thirds of the way through
    the baking time and bake the loaf directly on the stone. (Smaller or
    larger loaves will require adjustments in resting and baking time.)

10. Allow the bread to cool on a rack before slicing.

Gluten-Free Brioche

This recipe is dynamite baked as a traditionally shaped brioche or as a sandwich loaf for your kids' lunches. It has a soft texture with a light sweetness from the honey and vanilla that is pure comfort food. It can also be used in place of the brioche dough in Chapter 11 for many of the pastries in that chapter. A word about coconut oil in this recipe: if you use it, be aware that the dough will seem a little drier, but it bakes up beautifully and the flavor is fantastic.

Makes enough dough for at least three 1½-pound loaves. The recipe can be doubled or halved.

Ingredient	Volume (U.S.)	Weight (U.S.)	Weight (Metric)
Brown rice flour	1 cup	5⅓ ounces	150 grams
Tapioca flour (tapioca starch)	1 cup	4½ ounces	130 grams
Cornstarch	3¾ cups	1 pound, 3 ounces	535 grams
Granulated yeast	2 tablespoons	0.7 ounce	20 grams
Kosher salt[1]	1 tablespoon	0.6 ounce	15 grams
Xanthan gum or ground psyllium husk[2]	2 tablespoons	¾ ounce	20 grams
Milk	2½ cups	1 pound, 4 ounces	565 grams
Honey	1 cup	12 ounces	340 grams
Large eggs at room temperature, lightly beaten	4	8 ounces	225 grams
Oil (see page 21 for options) or melted unsalted butter	1 cup	7½ ounces	215 grams

Vanilla, pure extract	1 tablespoon	½ ounce	15 grams
Egg wash (see sidebar, page 189), for brushing on the loaf			
Raw sugar, for sprinkling on top crust			

[1]Can adjust to taste (see page 20).
[2]Double quantity if using psyllium.

1. **Mixing and storing the dough:** Whisk together the flour, tapioca starch, cornstarch, yeast, salt, and xanthan gum in a 6-quart bowl or a lidded (not airtight) food container.

2. Combine the liquid ingredients and gradually mix them into the dry ingredients, using a spoon or a heavy-duty stand mixer (with the paddle/flat beater), until all the dry ingredients are well incorporated. *We highly recommend the mixer for gluten-free doughs.*

3. Cover (not airtight), and allow the dough to rest at room temperature for approximately 2 hours.

4. The dough can be used immediately after its initial rise. Refrigerate it in a lidded (not airtight) container and use over the next 5 days. Freeze (airtight) if you're keeping it longer than that.

5. Grease a brioche pan or an 8½ × 4½-inch nonstick loaf pan. Use wet hands to break off a 1½-pound (small cantaloupe–size) piece of the refrigerated dough. Quickly pat it into a ball; this dough isn't stretched because there is no gluten in it—just gently press it into the shape. You might need to wet your hands a little more to prevent the dough from sticking and to create a smooth surface, but don't use so much water as to make the dough soggy.

6. Shape into a ball or oval, depending on your pan shape. Place it in the pan and allow to rest, loosely covered with plastic wrap, for 90 minutes (40 minutes if you're using fresh, unrefrigerated dough).

7. **Preheat the oven to 350°F.** A baking stone is not required, and omitting it shortens the preheat.

8. Just before baking, use a pastry brush to brush the top of the loaf with egg wash and sprinkle it with raw sugar.

9. Bake near the center of the oven for 40 to 45 minutes. The loaf is done when caramel brown and firm. (Smaller or larger loaves will require adjustments in resting and baking time.)

10. Remove the brioche from the pan and allow it to cool on a rack before slicing.

Gluten-Free Pizza with Fresh Mozzarella, Olives, Basil, and Anaheim Peppers (or Plain Pita!)

The secret to making really good gluten-free pizza is a thin crust! The technique is very different from wheat-based pizza, but once you get the hang of it, it won't be any more difficult. This is a very versatile method—if you don't use toppings, you get a gluten-free pita bread.

Makes one 12- to 16-inch pizza or pita; serves 4 to 6

½ pound (orange-size portion) Gluten-Free Crusty Boule dough (page 173), or Not Rye, mixed without caraway seeds (page 177)
White or brown rice flour for dusting

Pizza Toppings
⅓ cup (3 ounces/85 grams) tomato topping (see sidebar, page 159)
3 ounces (85 grams) fresh mozzarella cheese, cut into ½-inch chunks
6 fresh basil leaves, roughly torn
⅛ cup sliced Mediterranean-style black or green olives
½ Anaheim pepper, thinly sliced crosswise

1. **Thirty minutes before baking time, preheat the oven to 550°F (500°F for pita),** with a baking stone placed on the middle rack. You won't be using steam, so you can omit the broiler tray.

2. Prepare and measure all toppings in advance. The key to a pizza that slides right off the peel is to work quickly—don't let the dough sit on the peel any longer than necessary.

3. Dust the surface of the refrigerated dough with rice flour and cut off a ½-pound (orange-size) piece. Dust the piece with more rice flour and

🌀

Parchment makes it easier: Roll out gluten-free dough for pizza between a piece of lightly oiled parchment paper and plastic wrap. Peel up the oiled plastic wrap, top the dough, and bake right on the parchment paper. If the bottom isn't crisping enough, pull the paper out from under the dough after about 10 minutes.

quickly shape it into a ball; this dough isn't stretched because there is no gluten in it—just press it into the shape of a ball. You will need to use lots of rice flour to prevent the dough from sticking to your hands or the work surface, but avoid working lumps of flour into the dough.

4. Flatten the dough with your hands and a rolling pin directly on a wooden pizza peel to produce a $1/16$- to $1/8$-inch-thick round, dusting with lots of rice flour to keep the dough from sticking to the rolling pin and board (see sidebar). A metal dough scraper is very helpful here; use it to scrape the expanding dough round off the work surface when it sticks. Be sure that the dough is still movable before adding the toppings; if it isn't, sprinkle more rice flour under the dough.

5. **For pita, skip to Step 8 (with oven at 500°F).**

6. Distribute a thin layer of tomato topping over the surface of the dough.

7. Scatter the mozzarella over the surface of the dough, then the basil, olives, and pepper. No further resting is needed prior to baking.

8. Slide directly onto the stone (it may take a number of back-and-forth shakes to dislodge—use the dough scraper to help). Check for done-

ness in 10 to 12 minutes (5 to 6 for pita); turn in the oven if one side is browning faster than the other. It may need 5 more minutes in the oven, or until the cheese and crust are nicely browned. Pita should be removed before there's much browning.

9. Allow to cool slightly on a rack before serving (if you made pita, wrap it in clean towels to keep it soft).

11

ENRICHED BREADS AND PASTRIES

Wm'ere pleased to present great sweet enriched breads and pastries made from stored dough that keeps in the refrigerator for up to five days. If you keep enriched dough in your freezer, you'll be able to store it for weeks. Then, you can create terrific morning pastries, coffee cakes, holiday breads, and late-night chocolate fixes on the spur of the moment. Though some of them need a few minutes more preparation than our regular breads, they're all based on dough that will be stored, so the preparation time will be a fraction of what you've been used to with traditional pastries.

Challah

This is the braided eggy bread traditionally served in Jewish households at the start of the Sabbath on Friday nights (see color photo), but there's pretty much universal love here. Variations of an egg-enriched sweet loaf appear across bread-loving cultures. The choice of melted butter versus oil definitely changes the flavor and aroma, and families that observe Jewish dietary laws will match their choice to what's in their meal (meat, dairy, or neutral).

Our original challah recipe called for all-purpose flour, which most everyone has in the house. But some readers missed the highly defined braids and the ability to create fun shapes with stiffer dough, so we've given an option for using bread flour as well.

Makes four 1-pound loaves. The recipe can be doubled or halved.

Ingredient	Volume (U.S.)	Weight (U.S.)	Weight (Metric)
Lukewarm water (100°F or below)	1¾ cups	14 ounces	400 grams
Granulated yeast[1]	1 tablespoon	0.35 ounce	10 grams
Kosher salt[1]	1 to 1½ tablespoons	0.6 to 0.9 ounce	17 to 25 grams
Large eggs at room temperature, lightly beaten	4	8 ounces	225 grams
Honey	½ cup	6 ounces	170 grams
Oil (see page 21 for options) or melted unsalted butter	½ cup	4 ounces	115 grams
All-purpose flour (or substitute bread flour for a firmer dough)	7 cups	2 pounds, 3 ounces	990 grams
Egg wash (see sidebar, opposite), for brushing the loaf			
Poppy or sesame seeds, for sprinkling on top crust			
Oil, unsalted butter, or parchment paper, for the baking sheet			

[1]Can adjust to taste (see pages 18 and 20).

1. **Mixing and storing the dough:** Mix the yeast, salt, eggs, honey, and oil or melted butter with the water in a 6-quart bowl or a lidded (not airtight) food container.

2. Mix in the flour without kneading, using a spoon or a heavy-duty stand

∞

Egg wash—many ways: The standard is 1 egg lightly beaten with 1 tablespoon of water, but for a super-rich and dark caramel color on your loaf, use an egg yolk–only wash. You can mix it with cream for an even more dramatic color. For a super-outrageous finish, add a pinch of sugar or honey. Finally, if you are looking for shine but not a deep color, use an egg white–only wash, mixed with water. In all cases, you will combine one egg, one yolk, or one white with 1 tablespoon of liquid and whisk with a fork to break up the egg, so you don't end up having bits of egg cooked on the crust. Water-based egg wash freezes nicely in small jars for up to six weeks, defrosting overnight in the fridge. Shake well before using.

And if you ran out of eggs by putting them all into your challah dough, **you can use water to stick the seeds onto the loaf.** It won't be shiny or deeply brown, but the challah will still be delicious.

mixer (with the paddle/flat beater). If you're not using a machine, you may need to use wet hands to incorporate the last bit of flour.

3. Cover (not airtight) and allow to rest at room temperature until the dough rises and collapses (or flattens on top), approximately 2 hours.

4. The dough can be used immediately after the initial rise, though it is easier to handle when cold. Refrigerate the container of dough and use over the next 5 days. Beyond 5 days, freeze in 1-pound portions in an airtight container for up to 3 weeks. Defrost frozen dough overnight in the refrigerator before using, then allow the usual rest and rise time.

Visit BreadIn5.com, where you'll find recipes, photos, videos, and instructional material.

5. Grease or butter a baking sheet or line it with parchment paper or a silicone mat. Dust the surface of the refrigerated dough with flour and cut off a 1-pound (grapefruit-size) piece. Dust the piece with more flour and quickly shape it into a ball by stretching the surface of the dough around to the bottom on all four sides, rotating the ball a quarter-turn as you go.

6. Gently roll and stretch the dough, dusting with flour so your hands don't stick to it, until you have a long rope about ¾ inch thick. You may need to let the dough relax for 5 minutes so it won't resist your efforts. Using a dough scraper or knife, make angled cuts to divide the rope into 3 equal-length strands with tapering ends.

7. **Braiding the challah:** Starting from the middle of the loaf, pull the left strand over the center strand and lay it down; always pull the outer strands into the middle, never moving what becomes the center strand.

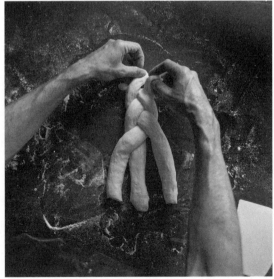

8. Now pull the right strand over the center strand. Continue, alternating outer strands but always pulling into the center. When you reach the end, pinch the strands together (see photos).

> ⌒◊
>
> **Braiding from one end:** You can braid starting at the end of the loaf and go all the way to the other end, but starting in the middle (and flipping) makes for a more even loaf.

9. Flip the challah over so that the loose strands fan toward you. Start braiding again by pulling an outside strand to the middle, but this time *start with the right strand*. Braid to the end again, and pinch the strands together.

10. If the braid is oddly shaped, fix it by nudging and stretching. Place on the prepared baking sheet and allow to rest for 90 minutes (see sidebar, page 70).

11. **Preheat the oven to 350°F.** A baking stone is not required, and omitting it shortens the preheat. Just before baking, use a pastry brush to brush the top of the loaf with egg wash and sprinkle with seeds.

12. Bake near the middle of the oven for about 30 minutes. (Smaller or larger loaves will require adjustments in baking time.) The challah is done when golden brown, and the braids near the center of the loaf offer resistance to pressure. Don't over-bake or you risk dryness. Due to the fat in the dough, challah will not form a hard, crackling crust.

13. Allow to cool on a rack before slicing and eating.

VARIATION: WHOLE WHEAT CHALLAH

Swap in 1½ cups of whole wheat flour for an equal amount of all-purpose (white) flour. No water adjustment is needed unless you push the whole wheat proportion beyond this, or if your whole wheat flour is particularly high in protein and your dough seems dry. If so, increase the water to produce a workable high-moisture dough (get familiar with our method before attempting).

VARIATION: APPLES AND HONEY CHALLAH

Core 2 large peeled or unpeeled baking apples and cut into ¼-inch dice. Add with the liquid ingredients; the apples work well with white or whole wheat challah (see color photo).

Turban-Shaped Challah with Raisins

A turban-shaped challah (see color photo) is served at the Jewish New Year. We've assumed in this recipe that you're using stored dough and rolling the raisins into it. If you're starting a batch of dough just for raisin challah, add a cup of raisins to the yeasted water when mixing.

Makes 1 round raisin challah

Parchment paper, silicone mat, unsalted butter, or oil, for the baking sheet
1 pound (grapefruit-size portion) Challah (page 187) or Brioche (page 195) dough
¼ cup raisins
Egg wash (see sidebar, page 189), for brushing the loaf
Sesame seeds, for sprinkling the top crust

1. Line a baking sheet with parchment paper or a silicone mat, or grease with butter or oil. Dust the surface of the refrigerated dough with flour and cut off a 1-pound (grapefruit-size) piece. Dust the piece with more flour and quickly shape it into a ball by stretching the surface of the dough around to the bottom on all four sides, rotating the ball a quarter-turn as you go.

2. Using a rolling pin and minimal dusting flour, roll out the dough to a thickness of ½ inch. Sprinkle with the raisins and roll into a log.

3. Rolling the dough between your hands and stretching it, form a single long, thin rope, tapering it at one end. If the dough resists shaping, let it rest for 5 minutes and try again.

4. Starting with the thick end of the rope, begin forming a coil on the prepared baking sheet. When you have finished coiling, pinch the thin end under the loaf. Allow to rest for 90 minutes loosely covered with plastic.

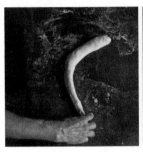

5. **Preheat the oven to 350°F.** A baking stone is not required, and omitting it shortens the preheat. Just before baking, use a pastry brush to brush the top of the loaf with egg wash, and sprinkle with seeds. Place in the center of the oven.

6. Bake for about 30 minutes. The challah is done when golden brown and the center of the loaf offers resistance to pressure. Due to the fat in the dough, challah will not form a hard, crackling crust.

7. Allow to cool on a rack before slicing and eating.

Brioche

Brioche originated in the Middle Ages in Normandy, France, a region long famed for its delicious butter. Don't be alarmed at the amount of butter in the recipe; brioche is supposed to be rich and indulgent, a great addition at brunches and holiday dinners or just as sandwich bread. The name "brioche" comes from the French word *broyer*, meaning to crush or grind, due to the excessive kneading required by the traditional dough—as much as 45 minutes in some recipes. Of course, with our version, we keep it to a few seconds, or you can skip the kneading altogether and have a warm loaf of brioche ready in no time flat.

Given all the eggs in this recipe, let them come to room temperature before using; otherwise, the rising will be slow.

Makes enough dough for at least three 1½-pound loaves. The recipe can be doubled or halved.

Ingredient	Volume (U.S.)	Weight (U.S.)	Weight (Metric)
Lukewarm water (100°F or below)	1½ cups	12 ounces	340 grams
Granulated yeast[1]	1 tablespoon	0.35 ounce	10 grams
Kosher salt[1]	1 tablespoon	0.6 ounce	17 grams
Large eggs at room temperature, lightly beaten	6	12 ounces	340 grams
Honey	½ cup	6 ounces	170 grams
Unsalted butter, melted, plus butter for greasing the pan	1½ cups (3 sticks)	12 ounces	340 grams

All-purpose flour	7 cups	2 pounds, 3 ounces	990 grams
Egg wash (see sidebar, page 189), for brushing the loaf			

[1]Can adjust to taste (see pages 18 and 20).

1. **Mixing and storing the dough:** Mix the water, yeast, salt, eggs, honey, and melted butter in a 6-quart bowl or a lidded (not airtight) food container.

2. Mix in the flour without kneading, using a Danish dough whisk, a spoon, or a heavy-duty stand mixer (with the paddle/flat beater). If you're not using a machine, you may need to use wet hands to incorporate the last bit of flour. The dough will be loose but will firm up when chilled; don't try to work with it before chilling.

3. Cover (not airtight), allow to rest at room temperature for 2 hours, and then refrigerate.

4. The dough can be used as soon as it's thoroughly chilled, at least 3 hours. Refrigerate the container and use over the next 5 days. Freeze (airtight) if you're keeping it longer than that.

5. Grease an 8½ × 4½-inch nonstick loaf pan generously with butter. Dust the surface of the refrigerated dough with flour and cut off a 1½-pound (small cantaloupe–size) piece. Dust the piece with more flour and quickly shape it into a ball, then elongating into an oval.

6. Place in the prepared pan. Cover loosely with plastic wrap and allow to rest for 90 minutes.

7. **Preheat the oven to 350°F,** with a rack placed in the center of the oven. A baking stone is not required, and omitting it shortens the preheat.

8. Just before baking, use a pastry brush to brush the top of the loaf with egg wash.

9. Bake for about 45 minutes, or until medium golden brown and well set.

10. Allow to cool on a rack before slicing.

ၑဢ

Dare we suggest kneading? Yes, we said the dreaded *K* word. Because brioche is intended to have a tighter crumb than regular breads, a little kneading won't harm things, as long as you do it *before* the first rise, and not when you shape the loaves. To get a bit more stretch in this dough, you can knead for as little as 30 seconds to really improve the texture. Just fold the dough over on itself several times on a floured surface, using the ball of your hand. The dough may need to rest for 10 minutes before you can roll it out easily, if rolling is required.

Brioche à Tête

Brioche à tête is a traditional French bread loaf, baked in a beautifully fluted pan and sporting an extra little ball of dough at the top (the tête, or head—see color photo). Your guests will think you slaved over this one. The shape is ubiquitous in Parisian shops but quite rare elsewhere.

Makes 1 loaf

1 pound (grapefruit-size portion) Brioche dough (page 195)
Butter or oil, for greasing the pan
Egg wash (see sidebar, page 189), for brushing the loaf

1. Grease an 8-inch fluted brioche pan.

2. Dust the surface of the refrigerated dough with flour and cut off a 1-pound (grapefruit-size) piece. Break off about an eighth of the dough to form the tête (head) and set it aside. Dust the large piece with more flour and quickly shape it into a ball by stretching the surface of the dough around to the bottom on all four sides, rotating the ball a quarter-turn as you go.

3. Place the larger ball in the prepared pan, seam side down; the pan should be about half full. Poke a fairly deep indentation in the top of this ball of dough. This is where you will attach the tête.

4. Quickly shape the small piece into a teardrop shape by rounding one end and tapering the other. Place the teardrop, pointed side down, into the indentation of the dough in the pan and pinch the two together gently but firmly to ensure the tête stays attached during baking.

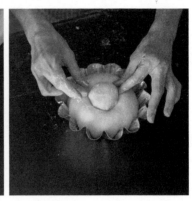

5. Allow to rest for 90 minutes, loosely covered with plastic wrap.

6. Preheat the oven to 350°F. A baking stone is not required, and omitting it shortens the preheat.

7. Using a pastry brush, paint the loaf with egg wash and place it in the center of the oven. Bake for about 40 minutes, or until golden brown and well set. (Smaller or larger loaves will require adjustments in resting and baking times.)

8. Immediately remove from the pan and allow to cool on a rack before serving.

Visit BreadIn5.com, where you'll find recipes, photos, videos, and instructional material.

Whole Wheat Brioche

This is a healthier variation on our ultra-decadent brioche (page 195) using a balance of white and whole wheat flours. We've also reduced the butter without losing flavor. This recipe proves that you can celebrate special occasions without having to sacrifice a healthy diet, and it's a delicious way to sneak whole grains into kids' diets.

Because whole grains and butter can make this loaf a bit dense, we've added vital wheat gluten to maintain the stretch, strength, and structure of the dough. You can find vital wheat gluten in the baking section of most grocery stores (see page 13).

Makes enough dough for at least two 2-pound loaves. The recipe can be doubled or halved.

Ingredient	Volume (U.S.)	Weight (U.S.)	Weight (Metric)
Whole wheat flour	4 cups	1 pound, 2 ounces	515 grams
All-purpose flour	3 cups	15 ounces	425 grams
Granulated yeast[1]	1 tablespoon	0.35 ounce	10 grams
Kosher salt[1]	1 tablespoon	0.6 ounce	17 grams
Vital wheat gluten[2]	¼ cup	1½ ounces	40 grams
Lukewarm water (100°F or below)	2¼ cups	1 pound, 2 ounces	510 grams
Unsalted butter, melted, plus additional for greasing pan	12 tablespoons (1½ sticks)	6 ounces	170 grams
Large eggs at room temperature, lightly beaten	5	10 ounces	285 grams

Honey	¾ cup	9 ounces	255 grams
Egg wash (1 egg beaten with 1 tablespoon water), for brushing the loaf (see sidebar, page 189)			

[1] Can adjust to taste (see pages 18 and 20).
[2] If omitting vital wheat gluten, decrease water to 1¾ cups.

1. **Mixing and storing the dough:** Whisk together the flours, yeast, salt, and vital wheat gluten in a 6-quart bowl or a lidded (not airtight) food container.

2. Combine the liquid ingredients and mix them with the dry ingredients without kneading, using a heavy-duty stand mixer (with the paddle/flat beater), Danish dough whisk, or a spoon. You might need to use wet hands to get the last bit of flour to incorporate if you're not using a machine. The dough will be loose, but it will firm up when chilled. Don't try to use it without chilling.

3. Cover (not airtight), allow to rest at room temperature for 2 hours, then refrigerate.

4. The dough can be used as soon as it's thoroughly chilled, at least 3 hours. Refrigerate the container and use over the next 5 days. Freeze (airtight) if you're keeping it longer than that.

5. Grease a brioche pan or an 8½ × 4½-inch nonstick loaf pan generously with butter. Dust the surface of the refrigerated dough with flour and cut off a 2-pound (large cantaloupe–size) piece. Dust the piece with more flour, quickly shape into a ball, and elongate into an oval. Place the ball in the prepared pan, cover loosely with plastic wrap, and allow to rest at room temperature for 1 hour 45 minutes.

Visit BreadIn5.com, where you'll find recipes, photos, videos, and instructional material.

6. **Preheat the oven to 350°F,** with a rack placed in the center of the oven. A baking stone is not required, and omitting it shortens the preheat.

7. Just before baking, use a pastry brush to brush the top of the loaf with egg wash.

8. Bake the loaf for about 50 minutes. (Smaller or larger loaves will require adjustments in resting and baking time.)

9. Remove the brioche from the pan (see sidebar, page 87) and allow it to cool on a rack before serving.

Wondrous Soft White Bread

There's just no substitute for the nostalgic and comforting taste of classic white bread—lightly enriched and sweetened. This recipe is perfect for re-creating the lunchbox sandwiches of childhood, only better, or making the golden-brown slice of toast with butter and jam that you've been craving. Just indulgent enough to be a treat, but simple enough to serve at any meal, this bread is sure to be an all-around family favorite. Because the dough's a little drier and firmer than our standard Master dough recipes, it holds its shape nicely for egg-free versions of Sticky Caramel Rolls (page 205), Raspberry Star Bread (page 222), Monkey Bread (page 224), or Raspberry Braid (page 219).

Makes enough dough for two 2-pound loaves. The recipe can be doubled or halved.

Ingredient	Volume (U.S.)	Weight (U.S.)	Weight (Metric)
Lukewarm water (100°F or below)	3 cups	1 pound, 8 ounces	680 grams
Granulated yeast[1]	1 tablespoon	0.35 ounce	10 grams
Kosher salt[1]	1 to 1½ table-spoons	0.6 to 0.9 ounce	17 to 25 grams
Sugar	⅓ cup	3 ounces	85 grams
Oil	¼ cup	2 ounces	60 grams
All-purpose flour	7½ cups	2 pounds, 5½ ounces	1,065 grams
Butter, for greasing the pan			
Egg wash (see sidebar, page 189), for brushing the loaf			

[1]Can adjust to taste (see pages 18 and 20).

1. **Mixing and storing the dough:** Mix the yeast, salt, sugar, and oil with the water in a 6-quart bowl, or a lidded (not airtight) food container.

2. Mix in the flour without kneading, using a spoon or a heavy-duty stand mixer (with the paddle/flat beater). If you're not using a machine, you may need to use wet hands to incorporate the last bit of flour.

3. Cover (not airtight), and allow to rest at room temperature for 2 hours, then refrigerate.

4. The dough can be used as soon as it's thoroughly chilled, at least 3 hours. Refrigerate the container and use over the next 5 days. Freeze (airtight) if you're keeping it longer than that.

5. Grease an 8½ × 4½-inch nonstick loaf pan generously with butter. Dust the surface of the refrigerated dough with flour and cut off a 2-pound (large cantaloupe–size) piece. Dust the piece with more flour, quickly shape into a ball, and elongate into an oval.

6. Place in the prepared pan. Allow to rest for 90 minutes, loosely covered with plastic wrap.

7. **Preheat the oven to 350°F.** A baking stone is not required, and omitting it shortens the preheat.

8. Use a pastry brush to brush the top of the loaf with egg wash just before baking.

9. Place the pan near the center of the oven and bake for 55 minutes, or until medium golden brown and well set.

10. Allow to cool completely on a rack before slicing.

Sticky Caramel Rolls—With or Without Nuts

This is probably our most popular sweet bread from past books. This recipe makes a big batch because if you don't make a bunch of them, you'll end up regretting it. Make sure you have a deep-enough pan or your caramel will try to escape: we recommend a 9-inch springform pan because it's deeper than a regular cake pan. You won't actually use the spring action unless the rolls get stuck, but they rarely do. We went a little crazy with the nuts, using 2 cups of a mix of almonds, pecans, and walnuts, but you can use any mix you want, or stick to just one kind (pecans are traditional). And if you're not a nut eater, you can skip them! (See color photo.)

Makes 8 large caramel rolls

12 tablespoons (1½ sticks) unsalted butter, melted, plus more for greasing
 the pan
1¼ cups well-packed brown sugar
¼ cup honey
1 teaspoon ground cinnamon
¼ teaspoon freshly grated nutmeg
½ teaspoon salt
Pinch freshly ground black pepper
⅔ cup pecan halves, toasted (optional)
⅔ cup walnut halves, toasted (optional)
⅔ cup whole almonds, toasted (optional)
1½ pounds (small cantaloupe–size portion) enriched dough (pages 187, 195,
 200, or 203)
All-purpose flour, for dusting

1. Mix together the melted butter, brown sugar, honey, cinnamon, nutmeg, salt, and pepper. Grease the sides of a 9 × 3-inch springform cake

pan with butter. (If your pan doesn't have a great seal, line the bottom and sides of the pan with a piece of parchment paper and grease the parchment.) Spread half the butter-sugar mixture evenly over the bottom. Scatter half the pecans, walnuts, and almonds (if using) over the butter-sugar mixture and set aside.

2. Dust the surface of the refrigerated dough with flour and cut off a 1½-pound (small cantaloupe–size) piece. Dust the piece with more flour and quickly shape it into a ball by stretching the surface of the dough around to the bottom on all four sides, rotating the ball a quarter-turn as you go.

3. Using a rolling pin, roll the dough out into a ⅛-inch-thick rectangle, about 8 × 14 inches. As you roll out the dough, use enough flour to prevent it from sticking to the work surface, but not so much as to make the dough dry. Spread the remaining butter-sugar mixture evenly over the rolled-out dough, chop the remaining nuts (if using), and sprinkle them over the top. Starting with the long side, roll the dough into a log and pinch the seam shut.

4. With a very sharp serrated knife or kitchen shears, cut the log into 8 equal pieces and arrange over the nuts in the pan, so the swirled cut edge is facing down. Cover loosely with plastic wrap and allow to rest for 1 hour.

5. **Preheat the oven to 350°F,** with a rack placed in the center of the oven.

6. Place the pan on a baking sheet, in case the caramel bubbles over, and bake for about 40 minutes, or until golden brown and well set in the center. While still hot, run a knife around the edge of the pan to release the rolls and invert immediately onto a serving dish. **If you let them set too long in the pan, they will stick and be difficult to turn out.**

7. Allow to cool for about 15 minutes before serving.

Refrigerator rise: Set your caramel rolls up the night before, so you can bake them first thing in the morning: Prepare the rolls, cover loosely with plastic wrap, and refrigerate for up to 18 hours. When ready to bake, preheat the oven, then slide in the rolls. They will take longer to bake, since they will be chilled. They've had a long, slow rise in the refrigerator, so you don't need to let them rise more before baking. This method works well for most of the breads in this book.

Cinnamon Rolls

Versions of the cinnamon roll can be traced to Denmark and Sweden, but they have taken on a life of their own in the United States. A day isn't complete without seeing the fluffy spiral buns, filled with cinnamon sugar and butter, slathered with icing, on Instagram. They've become synonymous with a joy-filled breakfast; a fresh batch is the perfect way to kick your mornings up a notch.

Makes 6 cinnamon rolls

The Cinnamon Rolls

1 pound (grapefruit-size portion) enriched dough (pages 187, 195, 200, or 203)

All-purpose flour, for dusting

2 tablespoons unsalted butter, melted (plus more for greasing the pan, if using one)

¼ cup granulated sugar

¼ cup well-packed brown sugar

Pinch salt

1½ teaspoons ground cinnamon (or add some zing and use Chinese five-spice powder instead)

½ teaspoon grated orange zest

The Cream Cheese Icing

4 ounces cream cheese, at room temperature

3 tablespoons confectioners' sugar

2 tablespoons heavy cream

½ teaspoon pure vanilla extract

¼ teaspoon grated orange zest

1. **Shape the cinnamon rolls:** Dust the surface of the refrigerated dough with flour and cut off a 1-pound (grapefruit-size) piece. Dust the piece with more flour and quickly shape it into a ball by stretching the surface of the dough around to the bottom on all four sides, rotating the ball a quarter-turn as you go.

2. Using a rolling pin, roll the dough out into a ¼-inch-thick rectangle, about 9 × 12 inches. As you roll out the dough, use just enough flour to prevent it from sticking to the work surface.

3. Brush the melted butter onto the entire surface.

4. In a small bowl, mix together the sugars, salt, cinnamon, and orange zest. Spread the mixture over the butter-topped dough. Use your hands to make sure you have an even coat of the sugar.

5. Roll the dough up, starting at a short end. Cut the log into 6 equal pieces.

6. Set the buns on a baking sheet lined with parchment paper or in a buttered 9-inch baking dish. If you're baking on a sheet, leave 1½ to 2 inches between them. It's okay if they touch in the oven.

7. Cover loosely with plastic wrap and allow to rest at room temperature for 75 minutes.

8. **Preheat the oven to 350°F,** with a rack placed in the center of the oven.

9. Bake for 25 to 30 minutes, or just until the centers are set when poked with your finger. They should be caramel colored.

10. Allow to cool for about 10 minutes.

11. **Prepare the cream cheese icing:** Mix together the ingredients for the icing and spread over the warm buns. Enjoy!

VARIATION: CROCK POT CINNAMON ROLLS

Follow the Cinnamon Rolls recipe but cut the log of dough into 8 pieces. Place the rolls close together on a piece of parchment paper and drop them into a crock pot. Cook on high for about an hour. Depending on your machine, it may take more or less time to cook. Cool and frost as directed (see page 105 for more on using the crock pot). Makes 8 rolls.

Sunny-Side-Up Apricot Pastry

This combination of buttery brioche dough, sweet vanilla pastry cream, and tart apricots masquerading as a sunny-side-up egg was made popular in Julia Child's book **Baking with Julia**. It's as fun to make and look at as it is to eat (see color photo).

Pastry cream is a staple in the pastry kitchen. To flavor this silky custard, you can use pure vanilla extract or try a vanilla bean, which gives the most intense flavor. To use the bean, just slice it lengthwise with a paring knife to expose the seeds. Scrape the seeds out of the pod and throw the seeds and the pod into your saucepan. The pod will get strained out at the end, leaving the fragrant aroma and the flecks of real vanilla behind.

Makes eight 4-inch pastries

The Pastry Cream (makes 3 cups)

2 cups whole milk

½ cup sugar

2 tablespoons unsalted butter

Pinch of salt

½ vanilla bean, split lengthwise and seeds scraped out, or 1 teaspoon pure vanilla extract

2 tablespoons cornstarch

1 large egg plus 3 large egg yolks

The Pastries

1½ pounds (small cantaloupe–size portion) enriched dough (pages 187, 195, 200, or 203)

All-purpose flour, for dusting

2 cups sugar

1 cup pastry cream (above)

---

8 ripe apricots, halved (fresh or canned)
½ cup apricot jam, melted

1. **Make the pastry cream:** Bring the milk, ¼ cup of the sugar, the butter, salt, and vanilla bean to a gentle boil in a medium-to-large saucepan. Remove from the heat and set aside to infuse.

2. Whisk together the cornstarch and the remaining ¼ cup sugar. Add the egg and egg yolks to the cornstarch and mix into a smooth paste.

3. Slowly, and in small amounts, whisk a little of the hot milk into the egg mixture to temper the eggs. Once the egg mixture is warm to the touch, pour it back into the milk in the pan.

4. Return the custard to the stovetop and bring to a boil, whisking continuously for 2 to 3 minutes, until thickened and the cornstarch is well cooked.

5. Strain the pastry cream into a shallow container and cover with plastic wrap, pressed directly on the surface to keep a skin from forming.

6. Set the container in the freezer for 15 minutes, just until chilled, then refrigerate.

7. **Make the pastries:** Line a baking sheet with parchment paper or a silicone mat.

8. Dust the surface of the refrigerated dough with flour and cut off a 1½-pound (small cantaloupe–size) piece. Dust the piece with more flour and quickly shape it into a rough ball by stretching the surface of the dough around to the bottom on all four sides, rotating the ball a quarter-turn as you go.

9. Using a rolling pin, roll the dough into a ¼-inch-thick rectangle, about 11 × 15 inches. As you roll out the dough, use just enough flour to prevent it from sticking to the work surface.

10. Using a round baking cutter, cut out eight 4-inch circles.

11. Cover the work surface with a generous coating of the sugar. Take one of the rounds and lay it in the sugar. Using a rolling pin and your fingers, roll back and forth over the center, stopping ½ inch from the 2 ends to create an oval. If the dough sticks to the rolling pin, dust the pin with a bit of flour. Lay the oval, sugar side up, on the lined baking sheet. Repeat with the rest of the dough, spacing the ovals at least 1 inch apart on the sheet.

12. Spread 2 tablespoons of the pastry cream in the center of each sugared oval. Place 2 apricot halves over the pastry cream so they resemble sunny-side-up eggs. Allow the pastry to rest for 45 minutes.

13. **Preheat the oven to 350°F.** A baking stone is not required, and omitting it shortens the preheat.

14. Bake the pastries in the center of the oven for about 30 to 35 minutes, or until the dough is golden brown and the sugar is nicely caramelized.

15. As soon as the pastries come out of the oven, brush the apricot jam over the pastries to give them a nice shine. Serve warm or cooled.

Honey-Glazed Doughnuts

The purest form of the doughnut, with nothing but a light honey glaze—because sometimes simplicity is best.

Makes twelve 3-inch doughnuts

The Doughnuts

1½ pounds (small cantaloupe–size portion) enriched dough (pages 187, 195, 200, or 203)

All-purpose flour, for dusting

Neutral-flavored oil, for frying (use oil with a high smoke point, like canola, peanut, or vegetable oil), enough to fill a deep saucepan to 3 inches from top

The Honey Glaze

2 cups confectioners' sugar

2 tablespoons honey

2 tablespoons heavy cream

¼ teaspoon pure vanilla extract

Pinch salt

1. **Prepare the doughnuts:** Dust the surface of the refrigerated dough with flour and cut off a 1½-pound (small cantaloupe–size) piece. Dust the piece with more flour and quickly shape it into a ball by stretching the surface of the dough around to the bottom on all four sides, rotating the ball a quarter-turn as you go.

2. Using a rolling pin, roll the dough out into a ¼-inch-thick rectangle, about 11 × 15 inches. As you roll out the dough, use just enough flour to prevent it from sticking to the work surface.

3. Have all of your equipment set out (see page 216). Heat the oil in a deep saucepan to 360°F–370°F, as determined by a candy thermometer (see sidebar on "Doughnut Frying" on page 216).

4. While the oil is heating, use a doughnut cutter to cut the dough into 12 circles. Reserve the centers to fry as well. Return any scraps to the bucket of dough.

5. Drop the doughnuts into the hot oil two or three at a time so that they have plenty of room; they'll sink and then rise to the surface, where they will remain. Be careful not to overcrowd them, or they will not rise nicely.

6. After 1 minute, gently flip the doughnuts over with a slotted spoon and fry for another minute or so, or until golden brown on both sides.

7. Remove the doughnuts from the oil and place them on paper towels to drain the extra oil. Repeat with the remaining dough until all the doughnuts are fried (you can also fry up the "holes").

8. **Prepare the honey glaze:** Combine the confectioners' sugar, honey, cream, vanilla, and salt in a bowl and stir until smooth. Dip the doughnuts in the glaze. You can eat them immediately or let the glaze set up firm while you brew your coffee. You're welcome!

EQUIPMENT FOR FRYING DOUGHNUTS

There are a few tools you'll need to make doughnuts. Nothing fancy, but having these on hand will make your doughnuts easier to make and as tasty as those from your favorite doughnut shop.

- A doughnut cutter or 3-inch and 1-inch round biscuit/cookie cutters (the little one is for the doughnut holes).

- A deep saucepan for frying the oil. It needs to be deep enough that your doughnuts can float in the oil without being too close to the rim of the pan. You want at least 3 inches above the oil to be safe.

- A candy thermometer for keeping track of oil temperature. Some people can look at the oil and know the temperature, but we like to use a thermometer.

- A slotted spoon or fry basket for retrieving the doughnuts from the hot oil.

- Paper towels, to absorb any excess oil from the fried doughnuts. Set the doughnuts on paper towels when they come out of the hot oil.

෧෨

The science of doughnut frying: Fried doughnuts don't become saturated with oil, so long as you fry them correctly. It's got to do with food's vapor pressure versus the oil's absorptive pressure, or to put it more plainly:

"If you fry at a high temperature (but not so high that it burns), the water inside the doughnut starts turning to steam immediately and pushes out through pores in the developing doughnut crust. That outward movement prevents inward movement of oil. If you keep the temperature right where Zoë recommends, the finished weight of the doughnut will be remarkably close to where you started—it won't absorb much oil. After weighing a bunch of doughnuts before and after frying, and accounting for up to a 10 percent water loss in finished baked goods, our best estimate is that each doughnut only absorbs between 15 and 45 calories' worth of oil." —Jeff

Visit BreadIn5.com, where you'll find recipes, photos, videos, and instructional material.

Jelly-Filled Doughnuts (Sufganiyot)

The Jewish holiday of Hanukkah commemorates an ancient miracle in which the oil lamp in Jerusalem remained ablaze for eight days despite only having a meager amount of fuel. This festival of lights is celebrated by burning candles against the darkness of winter and eating oil-fried foods. Our favorite is sufganiyot, jelly doughnuts smothered in confectioners' sugar. Small and delightful, they are the perfect end to a long winter evening.

Makes twelve 3-inch doughnuts

1½ pounds (small cantaloupe–size portion) enriched dough (pages 187, 195, 200, or 203)
All-purpose flour, for dusting
Vegetable oil, for frying
2 cups raspberry jam
Confectioners' sugar, for dusting, or flavored sugar (1 cup sugar mixed with ½ teaspoon lemon zest or cinnamon)

1. Follow the directions for the Honey-Glazed Doughnuts (page 214), but roll the dough ½ inch thick and don't cut a hole in the middle; just leave the circle of dough whole. Fry as directed.

2 Once the doughnuts are completely cool, poke the tip of a paring knife into one end to create a hole.

3. Fill a pastry bag, fitted with a large round pastry tip, with jam. Place the pastry tip in the doughnut and squeeze the jam into the center. You want enough jam so that every bite will have some, but not so much that it will explode when you eat it.

4. Dust with confectioners' or flavored sugar and serve.

Raspberry Braid

This braid is a showstopper and looks like you spent all day preparing it. The truth is, it's really easy and fast to make—the braid is a trick of the eye. This is the perfect sweet to bring to a brunch or book club, combining the brightness of raspberries with a creamy layer of lemony cheese filling (see color photo).

Makes 1 loaf

The Cream Cheese Filling
4 ounces cream cheese

1 tablespoon sugar

½ teaspoon grated lemon zest

The Braid
1 pound (grapefruit-size portion) enriched dough (pages 187, 195, 200, or 203)

All-purpose flour, for dusting

¾ cup raspberry jam

Egg wash (see sidebar, page 189), for brushing the loaf

The Raspberry Glaze
½ cup confectioners' sugar

2 tablespoons heavy cream (or more as needed to reach proper consistency)

6 ounces raspberries, for garnish and icing

1. **Prepare the cream cheese filling:** Mix the cream cheese, sugar, and lemon zest in a bowl until smooth. Set aside.

2. **Prepare the braid:** Line a baking sheet with parchment paper or a silicone mat.

3. Dust the surface of the refrigerated dough with flour and cut off a 1-pound (grapefruit–size) piece. Dust the piece with more flour and quickly shape it into a rough ball by stretching the surface of the dough around to the bottom on all four sides, rotating the ball a quarter-turn as you go.

4. Using a rolling pin, roll the dough out into a ¼-inch-thick rectangle, about 9 × 12 inches. As you roll out the dough, use just enough flour to prevent it from sticking to the work surface.

5. Lift the dough onto the lined baking sheet. Place the cream cheese filling down the length of the dough in a 1-inch strip in the center and add the raspberry jam on top.

6. Using a pizza cutter, cut about ½-inch-wide strips down each side. Twist and then fold the strips, left over right, crisscrossing over the filling. Lightly press the strips together as you move down the pastry, creating a braid. Cover loosely with plastic wrap and allow to rest at room temperature for 60 minutes.

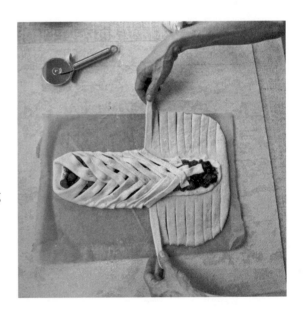

7. **Preheat the oven to 350°F,** with a rack placed in the center of the oven.

8. Use a pastry brush to brush lightly with egg wash just before baking.

9. Bake for 35 to 45 minutes, or until golden brown. Allow to cool.

10. **Prepare the raspberry glaze:** While the braid is cooling, mix together the confectioners' sugar and cream. Add enough cream so you can drizzle the glaze from a spoon.

11. Drizzle the braid with half the glaze, cover in raspberries, and drizzle with the remaining glaze.

Raspberry Star Bread

This very festive bread was a huge hit on our website, and it's an obvious choice for Christmas morning, since it looks just like an ornament (see photos at BreadIn5.com/StarBread). On the website, we used sugar and pumpkin pie spice, but here we enhanced the recipe with raspberry jam—you can get creative with all kinds of flavors.

Makes 1 large loaf

2 pounds (large cantaloupe–size portion) enriched dough (pages 187, 195, 200, or 203)
All-purpose flour, for dusting
1 cup raspberry jam
Egg wash (see sidebar, page 189), for brushing the loaf
Decorating sugar, for sprinkling on the loaf

1. Dust the surface of the refrigerated dough with flour and cut off a 2-pound (large cantaloupe–size) piece. Divide the piece into 4 equal pieces, dust with more flour, and quickly shape them into balls by stretching the surface of the dough around to the bottom on all four sides, rotating the ball a quarter-turn as you go.

2. Roll out the dough balls into 4 rounds about 10 inches wide. As you roll out the dough, add flour as needed to prevent sticking.

3. Place one of the dough rounds on a piece of parchment paper. Spread with one-third of the raspberry jam and top with a dough round. Spread with half of the remaining jam and top with another dough round, then spread with the remaining jam and top with the fourth dough round (photos of the process are at BreadIn5.com/StarBread).

4. Place a 2½-inch biscuit cutter (or similarly sized round template, like a juice glass) in the center of the dough. Leaving the biscuit cutter in place so you don't cut all the way to the center, use a knife or bench scraper to divide the circle into 16 equal sections.

5. Twist two of the sections away from each other with 2 rotations, then pinch the 2 sections together at the ends to form a point. Continue with the rest of the sections until you have 8 points.

6. Cover loosely with plastic wrap and allow to rest at room temperature for 90 minutes.

7. **Preheat the oven to 375°F,** with a rack placed in the center of the oven.

8. Transfer the parchment paper with the star onto a baking sheet. Use a pastry brush to brush the exposed dough with egg wash and sprinkle decorating sugar in the center of the loaf just before baking.

9. Bake for 25 to 30 minutes, or until golden brown and set.

10. Allow to cool on a rack before serving.

Monkey Bread

No one knows for sure how a cake made from caramelized blobs of dough got its whimsical name, but it seems fitting, considering that monkey bread lets everyone play with their food, tearing off chunks like monkeys. One thing is certain: This is not a dessert for people who take themselves too seriously! If you're anything like us, you'll want to start pulling apart this loaf as soon as it comes out of the oven, but give it just a minute to let the molten caramel cool down. This one is best served warm, while the caramel is still soft.

Makes 1 monkey bread

1½ pounds (small cantaloupe–size portion) enriched dough (pages 187, 195, 200, or 203)

All-purpose flour, for dusting

8 tablespoons (1 stick) unsalted butter, plus more for greasing the pan

1 cup granulated sugar

1 tablespoon plus 1 teaspoon ground cinnamon

2 tablespoons brown sugar

¼ teaspoon salt

1 teaspoon pure vanilla extract

1. Generously butter an 8½ × 4½-inch loaf pan or Bundt pan.

2. Dust the surface of the refrigerated dough with flour and cut off a 1½-pound (small cantaloupe–size) piece. Divide the dough into about 32 equal pieces. Roll the dough into small balls. If the dough sticks to your hands, coat your palms with a small amount of soft butter.

3. Melt 4 tablespoons butter in a bowl. Combine the granulated sugar and cinnamon in a second bowl. Drop the dough balls into the butter and then coat them with the cinnamon sugar.

4. Place the balls in the prepared pan and allow the loaf to rest for 60 minutes.

5. **Preheat the oven to 350°F,** with a rack placed in the center of the oven. A baking stone is not required, and omitting it shortens the preheat.

6. Just before putting the pan in the oven, melt the remaining 4 table-spoons butter, and then add any remaining cinnamon sugar, the brown sugar, the salt, and the vanilla. Pour over the dough balls.

7. Set the pan on a baking sheet, just in case the caramel bubbles over the top. Bake for about 40 minutes, or until caramelized and set. Allow the bread to cool for about 5 minutes.

8. Invert the loaf onto a serving tray and allow to cool slightly before serving.

Chocolate-Raisin Babka Bundt

It's not a typo—there really are sixteen yolks in this recipe, and we cut that back by half from the original Ukrainian recipe we were inspired by. This dough is super rich and decadent; it's best described as luxurious. You can make a twisted or Bundt-shaped babka by using any of our other doughs, but you should try this one on a special occasion.

Makes at least three 1½-pound loaves. The recipe can be doubled or halved.

Ingredient	Volume (U.S.)	Weight (U.S.)	Weight (Metric)
Lukewarm water (100°F or below)	3 cups	1 pound, 8 ounces	680 grams
Egg yolks at room temperature	16	1 pound	455 grams
Granulated yeast[1]	1 tablespoon	0.35 ounce	10 grams
Sugar	½ cup	3½ ounces	100 grams
Kosher salt[1]	1 tablespoon	0.6 ounce	17 grams
Unsalted butter, melted, plus more for greasing the pan	12 tablespoons (1½ sticks)	6 ounces	170 grams
All-purpose flour	7½ cups	2 pounds, 5½ ounces	1,065 grams
Bittersweet chocolate, melted, per loaf	¾ cup	4½ ounces	130 grams
Raisins, per loaf	¾ cup	4½ ounces	130 grams
Rum, for soaking the baked loaf (optional), per loaf	¼ cup	2 ounces	55 grams

[1]Can adjust to taste (see pages 18 and 20).

1. **Mixing and storing the dough:** Mix the water, egg yolks, yeast, sugar, salt, and melted butter in a 6-quart bowl or a lidded (not airtight) food container.

2. Mix in the flour without kneading, using a heavy-duty stand mixer (with the paddle/flat beater), a Danish dough whisk, or a spoon. The mixture will be quite loose because of all the yolks.

3. Cover (not airtight) and allow to rest at room temperature for 2 hours, until the dough rises.

4. The dough will be loose, but will firm up when chilled. Don't try to use it without chilling for at least 3 hours. Refrigerate the container and use over the next 5 days. Freeze (airtight) if you're keeping it longer than that.

5. Grease a Bundt pan or an 8½ × 4½-inch nonstick loaf pan with butter. Dust the surface of the refrigerated dough with flour and cut off a 1½-pound (small cantaloupe–size) piece. Dust the piece with more flour and quickly shape it into a ball by stretching the surface of the dough around to the bottom on all four sides, rotating the ball a quarter-turn as you go.

6. Using a rolling pin, roll the dough out into a ¼-inch-thick rectangle, about 11 × 15 inches. As you roll out the dough, use just enough flour to prevent it from sticking to the work surface. Spread the melted chocolate evenly over the dough and then sprinkle the raisins over it. Roll the dough into a log, starting at the long end, and pinch the seam closed.

7. Stretch the log until it is about 2 inches thick. Cut the log in half lengthwise. Twist the 2 long pieces together, always keeping the cut

side facing up. Form an oval, with the ends together, and place it in the prepared pan.

8. Cover loosely with plastic wrap and allow to rest at room temperature for 90 minutes.

9. **Preheat the oven to 350°F,** with a rack placed in the center of the oven. A baking stone is not required, and omitting it shortens the preheat.

10. Bake for 45 minutes, or until golden brown and firm. Brush with rum immediately (if using).

11. Allow to completely cool on a rack before serving.

Christmas Stollen

Our books are always published in late fall, just in time for holiday baking. Within days of the publication of our first book, we were inundated with requests for stollen, a German Christmas specialty rich with butter and eggs, spiced with cardamom, studded with dried and candied fruit, and spiked with just a touch of brandy. Here in Minnesota there is a large German-American population, and this festive bread is part of that tradition. It's gorgeous, with marzipan running through the middle. If you find the brandy a bit too festive, you can replace it with either orange juice or even black tea (see color photo). Note that you must make swaps/additions to the enriched dough of your choice as it's being mixed. Use the leftover dough for another purpose.

Makes one 1½-pound loaf

1½ pounds (small cantaloupe–size portion) enriched dough. Modify any
   enriched dough (pages 187, 195, 200, or 203) by swapping ¼ cup brandy,
   orange juice, or lukewarm black tea for ¼ cup of water in the full batch,
   and adding 1½ cups dried or candied fruit to the mixing liquid (raisins,
   currants, dried pineapple, dried apricots, dried cherries, candied citron,
   and/or candied lemon/orange peel. Use 1½ pounds of dough (small
   cantaloupe–size portion) for one stollen.
All-purpose flour, for dusting
½ cup marzipan, almond paste, or slivered almonds per loaf, for the center
Egg wash (see sidebar, page 189), for brushing the loaf
Confectioners' sugar, for sprinkling the top

1. Dust the surface of the refrigerated dough with flour and cut off a
    1½-pound (small cantaloupe–size) piece of dough. Dust the piece with
    more flour and quickly shape it into a ball.

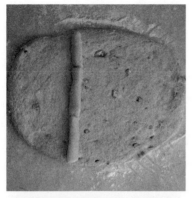

2. With a rolling pin, roll out the dough to a ¼-inch-thick oval. As you roll out the dough, use enough flour to prevent the dough from sticking to the work surface, but not so much as to make it dry.

3. Place marzipan, almond paste, or slivered almonds across the short end of the dough about one-third of the way from the end. Lift and fold the remaining two-thirds of the dough to form an S-shape over the almond filling. The end of the dough will lie near the middle of the top of the loaf. Allow to rest, loosely covered with plastic wrap, on a baking sheet prepared with parchment paper or a silicone mat, for 90 minutes.

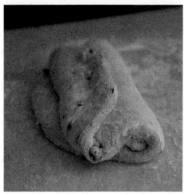

4. **Preheat the oven to 350°F,** with a rack placed in the center of the oven. If you're not using a stone in the oven, a 5-minute preheat is adequate.

5. Just before baking, use a pastry brush to brush the top of the loaf with egg wash.

6. Place the baking sheet in the oven and bake the stollen for 35 to 40 minutes, or until medium brown and firm.

7. Allow the stollen to cool, then sprinkle it generously with confectioners' sugar.

12

NATURAL SOURDOUGH STARTER (LEVAIN)

Master bread bakers believe that you can elevate breads to greatness by rising dough slowly with *levain* (starter), a bubbly mixture of flour, water, and naturally occurring microbes (wild yeast and bacteria). And when commercial yeast became difficult to find in 2020, people turned to natural sourdough to get their bread to rise. It takes some time to develop the *levain*, but once established it can be maintained indefinitely with very little effort, and it can be used in any of our recipes. **One word of advice: Don't try this until you're comfortable with our basic recipe in Chapter 5.** It's definitely more than five minutes of work and takes a little bread-baking experience, but not to worry—we'll walk you through each step in the process.

A wee bit of science: The microbes in levain come mostly from the flour, not from your local atmosphere. Traditional recipes have oversold the supposed regional magic that creates "San Francisco sourdough," or "Alaska sourdough." You should be able to make great sourdough in Des Moines, Phoenix, Minneapolis, or New York City.

Making your own new starter from scratch takes at least five days (if all goes swimmingly well), but if you already have some starter, you can skip ahead to the recipe on page 238, activate your starter, and jump right in. To streamline the sourdough process, once things are established, we don't call for "feeding" the starter as often as is done in traditional recipes. Instead we "dry out" the starter between feedings so you don't have to feed more often than monthly.

You'll use the levain to make full batches of dough that can be stored and used for up to five days—it doesn't rise well beyond that. Also, understand that the large, open, and irregular hole structure associated with sourdough will only be apparent in un-stored dough, made with mature sourdough that's mixed with additional flour and water, allowed to rise, *and baked that same day.* You can store some of that mixed, risen dough, and bake for five subsequent days, but it will have a tighter, smaller, and more uniform hole structure (the flavor will still be great). Your levain will produce a bread of incredible depth, with sourdough characteristics that you can't quite get with packaged yeast. And if you've gotten this far in the book, we think you're ready to try it.

Starting the Levain (Natural Flour-and-Water Culture)

Ingredients

Flour, quantities as below: You can make levain with white (unbleached) flour (any type), but the process starts more reliably if you use at least some whole wheat or rye flour (the microorganisms are more concentrated in the exterior bran of the grain) or even all whole grains—this will get the starter going more reliably.

Water: Filtered water (or bottled) sometimes works better than tap water, especially if your local tap water is very high in chlorine. If you don't have filtered water, you can allow tap water to sit overnight in an open container and that should allow the chlorine to dissipate (see troubleshooting tips below).

1. **Day 1:** In a clean container, mix ½ cup flour (2½ ounces/70 grams) and ½ cup lukewarm water (4 ounces/115 grams)—it should have the consistency of thick pancake batter. Cover loosely and store at room temperature for 48 hours. Dark liquid will collect on top and continue throughout the process—this is normal; it's not mold. Consider doing the whole process in an oven with the light on, which creates a warmer environment for bakers who live in cool (or air-conditioned) climates. Another option: your furnace room.

2. **Days 3, 4, 5, and 6—"feeding" (expanding) the levain:** By about Day 3, bubbles will become visible, and the mixture will have a sour aroma that some people describe as pleasantly "barn-yardy." Once that happens, mix in ½ cup each of flour and water and then continue to store at room temperature. Within a half day of feeding, the levain should be bubbling nicely (see color photo). As you continue daily feeding on

ଡ୬

True *levain* contains no commercial yeast, but **for a shortcut, add a just a pinch of any granulated yeast** in Step 1. Purists will scoff, but we can't tell the difference in the baked loaves. After a few days, the added yeast will have died off, leaving only wild microbes that were present in the flours (and, to a lesser extent, in the air).

days 4, 5, and 6, consider transferring to a larger container as needed, or discard some if you're accumulating too much (the discard can be used in yeast-risen batches and adds wonderful flavor). If your levain "stalls," consider feeding it twice daily.

3. **Subsequent days—using the levain:** You can begin to use the levain in baking after feeding it several times to produce enough for your recipe (that's called "expanding" the starter). Before using, make sure that it's actively bubbling and puffy. To be absolutely sure that your starter is very active, check to see if a spoonful of it floats in water. Otherwise keep feeding for additional days. Ultimately, you'll need about 3 cups of activated starter (about 2 pounds) to mix up a full four-pound batch of dough, and you'll want at least 1 cup (11 ounces) more, to maintain the levain. Beyond that, you can discard any extra (or use in yeast-risen batches to add wonderful flavor).

∽

Are barnyards really "pleasant"? We talk about levain having a "pleasant" barnyardy smell, and there's no other way to describe it, even though people who know their barnyards disagree. Think of this as the sweet smell of hay plus the slight whiff of a farm animal (a recently bathed one). It really and truly should be pleasant smelling. **If at any point in the development of your levain it begins to smell bad, something's gone wrong—but you can fix it.** Just throw out three-quarters of your starter and use what remains to start a new, larger culture with the consistency of thick pancake batter. It will take a while to develop, but the new culture should get back on the right track.

4. **"Drying out":** Always save at least 1 cup of levain after using it in a dough batch to act as the "mother" of the next batch of levain. Then "dry it out" by mixing in enough flour to make it dry and almost (but not quite) crumbly—this preserves the culture and makes it unnecessary to do frequent "feedings"—and refrigerate. If you ever see mold on stored levain or dough, throw it out and start over (see page 53 for details on recognizing mold versus the typical and normal gray liquid that collects over stored dough or levain).

5. **Monthly feedings—or bringing "dried out" culture back to life ("activating" it):** Starting with 1 cup of dried-out sourdough culture (see Step 4), blend in 2 cups water and 2 cups flour; you may need a little more water to bring the mixture to the consistency of thick pancake batter. Cover loosely, then allow to ferment until bubbling and puffy. Expand the starter to make as much as you'll need for your batch, or "dry out" again for storage, discarding any that you don't need.

6. **You can freeze levain or mother culture:** If you don't have time to keep a mother culture alive in the refrigerator, it can be frozen. Traditional books suggest that the culture can't survive for longer than a few months at freezing temperature, but we've thawed and rejuvenated cultures that were frozen for over a year (it can take a number of feedings to wake it up).

∽

Mother culture: Any bit of sourdough that you use to start a new batch is traditionally called the "mother."

Tips if you're having trouble starting or maintaining active levain

If your starter is stalled and it isn't getting to the very active stage, if your loaves aren't rising well, or if they're too dense...

1. **Manage your expectations:** After incorporating starter into a dough and baking your first loaf, you should get the nice, open hole structure that is the hallmark of sourdough bread. If you're doing our stored-dough method, that same dough won't yield an "open" crumb on subsequent days. You'll get smaller, more uniform holes, but sourdough flavor will still be there (and will intensify over the five-day storage life of the batch).

2. **Increase the temperature:** Getting a starter to an active phase within a week or two requires a warm environment, and in cool weather, or anytime at all, you may have better results by storing the developing starter in the oven with the **heat off**, but with the **oven light on (alternative: your furnace room)**. Many people have better results starting new levain in the summer for this reason (but the problem, of course, is that we like to bake bread in the cool seasons).

3. **Be patient!** Depending on local conditions (especially cool temperatures), initial activation could require fourteen days of feeding, rather than seven. Most often, the process slows down around Day 4 or 5, so don't give up—keep feeding through those days. That said, if you do give up, the discarded levain-attempt can be incorporated into yeasted batches. **If at any stage dark liquid collects on top, don't worry about it. Just mix this in as you feed/expand your starter.**

4. **Feed/expand twice daily rather than once:** You'll be giving the growing microorganism colony more food to eat. If you increase the feedings, you'll need to discard one-third of the starter before feeding or you'll end up with too much. You can use excess starter in yeast-risen doughs, where they'll add flavor.

5. **Use whole grains:** You'll get more reliable start-up if you use at least some whole wheat or rye flour.

6. **Consider using filtered or bottled water:** If your local water supply is high in chlorine, that can inhibit wild yeast growth. Alternative: Let your tap water sit overnight in an open container, which dissipates the chlorine.

7. **Transfer to a clean jar for every feeding:** Contamination with poorly rising microorganisms could be the culprit in a slow-to-expand starter.

100% Levain-Risen Bread: White or Whole Wheat

This makes an incredibly flavorful loaf, one that many consider to be the holy grail of home bread baking. Just be sure you've mastered the regular yeast-risen Master Recipe in Chapter 5 before you tackle this one. In the ingredients list, we talk about the consistency (really, the hydration) of the levain, and this will very much affect how much water you need in your dough, so be ready to adjust water and flour to match the consistency of your Chapter 5 dough. You can use starter made from white, rye, or whole wheat flour, and use it in recipes where the primary flour is white, whole wheat, or bread flour. But a word of advice: start with loaves made mostly with white flour—they rise more reliably if your starter isn't quite as active as it should be. Whole grains require very, very active starter.

Makes enough dough for four 1-pound loaves. The recipe can be doubled or halved.

Ingredient	Volume (U.S.)	Weight (U.S.)	Weight (Metric)
Lukewarm water	1½ cups	12 ounces	340 grams
Kosher salt[1]	1 tablespoon	0.6 ounce	15 grams
Activated levain, the consistency of thick pancake batter	3 cups	2 pounds	910 grams
All-purpose flour[2]	6½ cups	2 pounds	910 grams
Cornmeal or parchment paper, for the pizza peel			

[1]Can adjust to taste (see page 20).
[2]Decrease to 6 cups if using whole wheat flour (1 pound, 11 ounces/765 grams), or 6¼ cups bread flour (31 ounces/875 grams). Measurements are approximate and depend on the hydration level of your active starter—adjust as needed.

1. **Mixing and storing the dough:** Mix the water and salt in a 6-quart bowl, or a lidded (not airtight) food container, then stir in the levain, using a fork to break it up.

2. Add the flour and mix without kneading, using a spoon or a heavy-duty stand mixer (with the paddle/flat beater). You may need extra flour or water to bring the dough to the consistency of our other recipes, depending on the water content of your levain (which is why we strongly recommend becoming very familiar with our doughs before trying this one).

3. Cover (not airtight), and allow the dough to rest at room temperature until it doubles in size. Depending on the condition of your levain and

---

∾

Using sourdough for flavor instead of leavening—in any of our recipes: If you don't want to go full bore into the world of sourdough baking, you can use levain as a flavoring agent, and packaged yeast as the leavening agent. Sourdough starter, after it's activated, is 35% to 40% water. Knowing that, you can add it to any recipe in this book: Add about 1½ cups (1 pound/455 grams) of activated sourdough starter to any of our full-batch recipes. Then decrease the water by ¾ cup, and the flour by ¾ cup. Adjust moisture levels and flour as needed.

You can also decrease the commercial yeast well below what we call for in any recipe (see page 18) **or omit it entirely** and use the full dose of starter, adjusting flour and water as needed. One word of advice—sourdough is an assertive flavor, and most of our taste testers didn't love it in challah or brioche.

---

the room temperature, this may be as fast as 2 hours, or it may take as long as 6 to 12 hours. This slow rise will contribute to the taste of authentic levain-risen bread.

4. The dough can be used immediately after the initial rise, though it is easier to handle when cold. Refrigerate it in a lidded (not airtight) container and use over the next 5 days, or freeze for up to 4 weeks.

5. Dust the surface of the refrigerated dough with flour and cut off a 1-pound (grapefruit-size) piece. Dust the piece with more flour and quickly shape it into a ball by stretching the surface of the dough around to the bottom on all four sides, rotating the ball a quarter-turn as you go.

6. Pat the ball into a narrow oval. Place the loaf on a pizza peel prepared
• with cornmeal or lined with parchment paper, cover loosely with plastic wrap or an overturned bowl, and allow to rest for 90 minutes (40 minutes if you're using fresh, unrefrigerated dough). Alternatively, you can rest the loaf on a silicone mat or greased baking sheet without using a pizza peel.

7. **Thirty minutes before baking time, preheat the oven to 450°F,** with a baking stone placed on the middle rack. Place an empty metal broiler tray on any other rack that won't interfere with the rising bread.

☙

You may need a longer resting time than usual, up to 2 or even 3 hours if the dough seems like it's very firm, or remains cold—the dough should feel relaxed and "jiggly" on the pizza peel.

8. Dust with flour and slash the loaf with ½-inch-deep parallel cuts, using a serrated bread knife (see photos, page 71).

9. Slide the loaf directly onto the hot stone (or place the silicone mat or baking sheet on the stone if you used one). Pour 1 cup of hot water into the broiler tray and quickly close the oven door (see page 28 for steam alternatives). Bake for about 30 minutes, or until richly browned and firm. If you used parchment paper, a silicone mat, or a baking sheet under the loaf, carefully remove it and bake the loaf directly on the stone or an oven rack two-thirds of the way through the baking time. (Smaller or larger loaves will require adjustments in resting and baking time.)

10. Allow the bread to cool on a rack before slicing.

VARIATION: SHORT-CUT LEVAIN LOAVES FROM YEASTED BATCHES

This is just a version of the Lazy Sourdough Shortcut (page 74)—all you need to do is use a lot of dough from your last batch, about 2 pounds (a half-batch), and use that to build a new full batch (halve the ingredients), without any added commercial yeast. It may take up to 48 hours for its initial rise. You can keep this up indefinitely if you continue to enjoy the flavor. Don't use dairy or other perishables in batches you handle this way.

A more structured whole wheat loaf with vital wheat gluten: To create a stronger whole wheat dough that's closer to the 100% Whole Wheat Dough in Chapter 6 (page 80), whisk ¼ cup (1⅜ ounces/40 grams) of vital wheat gluten into the flour before adding the dry ingredients to the liquids. You'll need to increase the water by about ½ cup.

SOURCES FOR BREAD-BAKING PRODUCTS

BreadIn5.com/equipment

Cooks of Crocus Hill (Minneapolis, St. Paul, and Stillwater, Minnesota): CooksOfCrocusHill.com, 612.223.8167, 651.228.1333, or 651.351.1144

King Arthur Baking Company: KingArthurBaking.com, 800.827.6836

Le Creuset cookware: LeCreuset.com, 877.418.5547

Lodge Cast Iron cookware: LodgeMfg.com, 423.837.7181

Penzeys Spices: Penzeys.com, 800.741.7787

Red Star Yeast: RedStarYeast.com, 800.445.5746

Tupperware: Tupperware.com, 800.366.3800

INDEX

aging dough, 52
air-insulated baking sheets, 34
alcohol aroma, 57
all-purpose flour, 11–12
  American-Style Whole Wheat Sandwich Bread, 134–136
  Brioche, 195–197
  Buttermilk Cinnamon-Raisin Bread, 143–145
  Challah, 187–192
  Chocolate-Raisin Babka Bundt, 226–228
  Deli-Style Rye Bread, 122–124
  European Peasant Bread, 117–119
  Light Whole Wheat Dough, 83–84
  master recipe, 63–64
  100% Levain-Risen Bread: White or Whole Wheat, 238–241
  Pain au Potiron (Peppery Pumpkin and Olive Oil Loaf), 140–142
  Pumpernickel Bread, 125–128
  Sticky Caramel Rolls—With or Without Nuts, 205–207
  Vermont Cheddar Bread, 137–139
  Whole Wheat Brioche, 200–202
  Wondrous Soft White Bread, 203–204
  Yeasted Thanksgiving Cornbread with Cranberries, 154–155
almonds/almond paste
  Christmas Stollen, 229–230
  Sticky Caramel Rolls—With or Without Nuts, 205–207
aluminum-foil roasting pans, 28–29, 59
American-Style Pizza, 161
American-Style Whole Wheat Sandwich Bread, 134–136
Apples and Honey Challah, 192
Apricot Pastry, Sunny-Side-Up, 211–213
artificial sweeteners, 24–25
avocado oil, 22

Baba Ghanoush, 103–104
Babka Bundt, Chocolate-Raisin, 226–228
Bagels, 146–148
Baguette, 88–91
Baguette Buns, 109–110
baguette pans, 34
baker's percentage, 42
baking sheets, 31, 34–35
baking stones, 72
baking stones/steels, 30–31, 54
baking times and temperatures, 6, 45–46
  See also tips and techniques
barley malt, 24
barnyard odor, 234
basic doughs
  Baguette, 88–91
  Bâtard, 94–95

basic doughs *(continued)*
Ciabatta, 96–97
Couronne, 98–99
Crock Pot Bread (Fast
Bread in a Slow
Cooker), 105–107
Crusty and Hearty White
Sandwich Loaf, 85–87
Garlic Knots with Parsley
and Olive Oil, 114–115
Light Whole Wheat Dough,
83–84
Olive Bread, 120–121
100% Whole Wheat
Dough, 79–81
Pain d'Épi, 92–93
Pita, 100–102
rolls and buns, 108–115
shaping techniques, 85–115
Bâtard, 94–95
bench knives, 33
bittersweet chocolate
Black-and-White Braided
Pumper-nickel and Rye
Loaf, 128
Chocolate-Raisin Babka
Bundt, 226–228
blind baking, 161–162
blobs, flour, 49
boiled doughs
Bagels, 146–148
Soft Pretzels, 150–153
boules, 63–76
braided breads
Black-and-White Braided
Pumpernickel and Rye
Loaf, 128
Challah, 187–192
Raspberry Braid, 219–221
brandy
Christmas Stollen, 229–230
bread flour, 12–13

bread knives, 36
brioche
Brioche, 195–197
Brioche à Tête, 198–199
Gluten-Free Brioche,
180–182
Whole Wheat Brioche,
200–202
brioche pans, 35
broiler trays, 28–29
Brötchen, 110–111
brown rice flour, 15–16
Gluten-Free Brioche,
180–182
Gluten-Free Crusty Boule,
173–175
Not Rye, But So Very
Close, 177–179
brown sugar, 23–24
buckets, 32–33
Bundt, Chocolate-Raisin
Babka, 226–228
buns, 108–115, 153
butter, 21, 82
Buttermilk Cinnamon-Raisin
Bread, 143–145

caramel coloring, 127
Caramel Rolls—With or
Without Nuts, Sticky,
205–207
caraway seeds, 23
Deli-Style Rye Bread,
122–124
Not Rye, But So Very
Close, 177–179
cassava, 16
cast-iron pizza pans/skillets,
30, 54, 86
ceramic baking stones, 30–31,
54
challah

Challah, 187–192
Turban-Shaped Challah
with Raisins, 193–194
Cheddar Bread, Vermont,
137–139
cheese
Gluten-Free Pizza with
Fresh Mozzarella,
Olives, Basil, and
Anaheim Peppers,
183–185
Pizza Margherita, 158–161
Vermont Cheddar Bread,
137–139
Cherry-Black Pepper
Focaccia, 165
chile peppers
Gluten-Free Pizza with
Fresh Mozzarella,
Olives, Basil, and
Anaheim Peppers,
183–185
Chocolate-Raisin Babka
Bundt, 226–228
Christmas Stollen, 229–230
Ciabatta, 96–97
cinnamon
Buttermilk Cinnamon-
Raisin Bread, 143–145
Cinnamon Rolls, 208–210
Monkey Bread, 224–225
Sticky Caramel Rolls—
With or Without Nuts,
205–207
clay bakers, 29
Cloverleaf Rolls, 111–112
cocoa powder
Pumpernickel Bread,
125–128
coconut oil, 22
confectioners' sugar, 24
containers, storage, 32–33

convection ovens, 38–39
conversion tables, 61
cooked pizza sauce, 159
cookie sheets, 34–35
cooling racks, 36
cornmeal, 16, 46–47
cornstarch, 16
    Gluten-Free Brioche,
        180–182
cornstarch wash, 121, 122
Couronne, 98–99
cracker crust pizzas, 161
Cranberries, Yeasted
    Thanksgiving
    Cornbread with,
    154–155
Cream Cheese Filling, 219–
    221
Cream Cheese Icing, 208–210
Crisp Cheesy Bread Sticks,
    139
crockery containers, 33
Crock Pot Bread (Fast Bread
    in a Slow Cooker),
    105–107
Crock Pot Cinnamon Rolls,
    210
crumb, 44–45, 47–49,
    51–52
Crusty and Hearty White
    Sandwich Loaf, 85–87
custard crumb, 44–45

Danish dough whisks, 36, 67
Date-and-Walnut Bread,
    Pumpernickel, 129–130
Deli-Style Rye Bread, 122–
    124
dense doughs, 51–52
digital scales, 37, 41–42
dough consistency, 43–44
doughnuts

frying tips and techniques,
    216–217
Honey-Glazed Doughnuts,
    214–215
Jelly-Filled Doughnuts
    (Sufganiyot), 218
dough scrapers, 33
dough whisks, 36, 67
dried fruit
    Cherry-Black Pepper
        Focaccia, 165
    Christmas Stollen, 229–230
    See also raisins
dry crumb, 49

eating tips, 50
eggplant
    Baba Ghanoush, 103–104
eggs, 20, 22
    Brioche, 195–197
    Challah, 187–192
    Chocolate-Raisin Babka
        Bundt, 226–228
    Gluten-Free Brioche,
        180–182
    Gluten-Free Crusty Boule,
        173–175
    Not Rye, But So Very
        Close, 177–179
    Whole Wheat Brioche,
        200–202
egg wash, 189
egg white–enriched dough,
    110–111
enriched breads and pastries,
    187, 224–225
    Brioche, 195–197
    Brioche à Tête, 198–199
    Challah, 187–192
    Chocolate-Raisin Babka
        Bundt, 226–228
    Christmas Stollen, 229–230

Cinnamon Rolls, 208–210
Honey-Glazed Doughnuts,
    214–215
Jelly-Filled Doughnuts
    (Sufganiyot), 218
Monkey Bread, 224–225
Onion Pletzel, 165
Raspberry Braid, 219–221
Raspberry Star Bread,
    222–223
Sticky Caramel Rolls—
    With or Without Nuts,
    205–207
Sunny-Side-Up Apricot
    Pastry, 211–213
Turban-Shaped Challah
    with Raisins, 193–194
Whole Wheat Brioche,
    200–202
Wondrous Soft White
    Bread, 203–204
enriched doughs, 55
equipment, 27–39
European Peasant dough
    Ciabatta, 96–97
    Couronne, 98–99
    Crock Pot Bread (Fast
        Bread in a Slow
        Cooker), 105–107
    Crusty and Hearty White
        Sandwich Loaf, 85–87
    European Peasant Bread,
        117–119
    Garlic Knots with Parsley
        and Olive Oil,
        114–115
    Olive Bread, 120–121
    Pita, 100–102
    rolls and buns, 108–113
    weights and measures, 118
exhaust fans, 161
expiration dates, 19

fermentation aromas, 57
filtered water, 17
flatbreads, 157
    Focaccia with Onion and
        Rosemary, 163–164
    Fougasse Stuffed with
        Roasted Red Pepper,
        168–170
    Olive Fougasse,
        166–167
    Pita, 100–102
    See also pizzas
flavor development, 43
flaxseed oil, 22
flour blobs, 49
flours, 11–15
Focaccia, Cherry-Black
    Pepper, 165
Focaccia with Onion and
    Rosemary, 163–164
food-grade storage containers,
    32–33
food-grade water sprayer
    bottles, 28
food processors and mixers,
    37–38, 67
Fougasse, Olive, 166–167
Fougasse Stuffed with
    Roasted Red Pepper,
    168–170
frequently asked questions
    (FAQs), 50–60
fresh bread storage, 55
frozen dough, 56–57

garlic, roasted, 104
glass containers, 33
gluten, 11–12, 14
    See also vital wheat gluten
gluten cloak, 51, 68–70
gluten-free flours/doughs,
    15–16

Gluten-Free Brioche,
    180–182
Gluten-Free Crusty Boule,
    173–175
Gluten-Free Pizza with
    Fresh Mozzarella,
    Olives, Basil, and
    Anaheim Peppers,
    183–185
Gluten-Free Sandwich
    Bread, 175–176
ingredients, 15–17
mixing tips, 49–50
Not Rye, But So Very
    Close, 177–179
tips and techniques, 171–
    172, 184
grains, 16
    See also rye flour; whole
    wheat flour/breads
grains as lubricants, 46–47
gray dough, 53
grilled breads, 58–59, 162
gummy crumb, 47–48

heavy doughs, 51–52
heavy-gauge baking sheets,
    31, 34–35, 72
herb breads, 75
high-altitude baking, 57–58
high-moisture doughs, 4–8,
    12, 43–44
honey, 24
    American-Style Whole
        Wheat Sandwich Bread,
        134–136
    Brioche, 195–197
    Challah, 187–192
    Gluten-Free Brioche,
        180–182
    Gluten-Free Crusty Boule,
        173–175

Honey-Glazed Doughnuts,
    214–215
Not Rye, But So Very
    Close, 177–179
100% Whole Wheat
    Sandwich Bread with
    Milk and Honey,
    131–133
Sticky Caramel Rolls—
    With or Without Nuts,
    205–207
Honey Whole Wheat Dough,
    81–82
hydration levels, 42

Icing, Cream Cheese, 208–
    210
immersion blenders, 38
ingredients, 11–25
instant-read thermometers,
    73
international breads
    Bagels, 146–148
    Deli-Style Rye Bread,
        122–124
    European Peasant Bread,
        117–119
    Olive Bread, 120–121
    Pain au Potiron (Peppery
        Pumpkin and Olive Oil
        Loaf), 140–142
    Pumpernickel Bread,
        125–128
    Soft Pretzels, 150–153

Jelly-Filled Doughnuts
    (Sufganiyot), 218
jelly-roll pans, 34–35

Kalamata olives
    Olive Fougasse, 166–167
kitchen shears/scissors, 37

kneading, 4–8, 197
Kosher salt, 20

lames, 36
Lazy Sourdough Shortcut, 74, 241
lean doughs, 55
letter-fold bread-shaping technique, 90
levain, 231–237, 239
Light Whole Wheat Dough, 83–84
liquid measures, 61
liquid sweeteners, 24
loaf pans, 35, 86, 87
lukewarm water, 17, 19
lye, 152

malt powder/syrup, 24, 146
manioc, 16
marzipan
    Christmas Stollen, 229–230
master recipe, 63–78
    Baguette, 88–91
    basic boule, 63–76
    Bâtard, 94–95
    Ciabatta, 96–97
    Couronne, 98–99
    Crock Pot Bread (Fast Bread in a Slow Cooker), 105–107
    Crusty and Hearty White Sandwich Loaf, 85–87
    forming and baking steps, 68–73
    Garlic Knots with Parsley and Olive Oil, 114–115
    Herb Dough, 75
    mixing and storing, 65–68, 78
    Olive Bread, 120–121
    Olive Oil Dough, 75–76

Pain d'Épi, 92–93
Pita, 100–102
rolls and buns, 108–115
shaping techniques, 85–115
Strong White Dough, 77–78
weights and measures, 64, 77
measuring cups, 37
measuring spoons, 37
measuring tips, 41–42
metal bowls, 28–29, 59
metric measures, 61
    See also weights and measures
microplane zesters, 38
milk
    Gluten-Free Brioche, 180–182
    100% Whole Wheat Sandwich Bread with Milk and Honey, 131–133
mini loaf pans, 35–36
moisture content, 43–44
molasses
    Not Rye, But So Very Close, 177–179
    Pumpernickel Bread, 125–128
moldy dough, 53
Monkey Bread, 224–225
Moon and Stars Bread, 95
mother culture, 235
mozzarella cheese
    Gluten-Free Pizza with Fresh Mozzarella, Olives, Basil, and Anaheim Peppers, 183–185
    Pizza Margherita, 158–161

neutral-flavored oils, 21–22

Non-Boiled Onion-Poppy Seed Bagels, 148–149
Not Rye, But So Very Close, 177–179
nutmeg
    Sticky Caramel Rolls— With or Without Nuts, 205–207
nuts, 23
    Pumpernickel Date-and- Walnut Bread, 129–130
    Sticky Caramel Rolls— With or Without Nuts, 205–207

odd-shaped loaves, 54–55
oils, 21–22, 82
olive oil, 22
    Garlic Knots with Parsley and Olive Oil, 114–115
Olive Oil Dough, 75–76
    Pain au Potiron (Peppery Pumpkin and Olive Oil Loaf), 140–142
olives
    Gluten-Free Pizza with Fresh Mozzarella, Olives, Basil, and Anaheim Peppers, 183–185
    Olive Bread, 120–121
    Olive Fougasse, 166–167
omitted steps, 6
100% Levain-Risen Bread: White or Whole Wheat, 238–241
100% Whole Grain Rye Dough, 81
100% Whole Wheat Dough, 79–82

100% Whole Wheat Sandwich Bread with Milk and Honey, 131–133
100% Whole Wheat with Oil, 82
Onion Pletzel, 165
orange zest
    Cinnamon Rolls, 208–210
    Yeasted Thanksgiving Cornbread with Cranberries, 154–155
organic flours, 15
oven spring, 5, 31, 43–44, 50–51
oven temperatures, 52, 61, 161
oven thermometers, 32
overbaking problems, 49

Pain au Potiron (Peppery Pumpkin and Olive Oil Loaf), 140–142
Pain d'Épi, 92–93
parbaked breads, 60
parchment paper, 34–35, 47, 184
Parsley and Olive Oil, Garlic Knots with, 114–115
pastry brushes, 38
Pastry Cream, 211–213
pecans
    Sticky Caramel Rolls—With or Without Nuts, 205–207
peels, 31, 46–47, 72
Peppery Pumpkin and Olive Oil Loaf, 140–142
Pita, 100–102, 162
pizza peels, 31, 46–47, 72
pizzas, 157
    Gluten-Free Pizza with

Fresh Mozzarella, Olives, Basil, and Anaheim Peppers, 183–185
Pizza Margherita, 158–161
variations, 161–162
pizza sauce, 159
pizza stones, 30
plastic storage containers, 32–33
poppy seeds, 23
    Bagels, 148
    Challah, 187–192
    Onion Pletzel, 165
powdered sugar, 24
preheating times, 54
pre-mixed doughs, 4–8
Pretzel Buns, 153
product sources, 243
proofing yeast, 6, 7, 19
protein content, 11–12
psyllium husk, 16–17
    Gluten-Free Brioche, 180–182
    Gluten-Free Crusty Boule, 173–175
    Not Rye, But So Very Close, 177–179
pull-apart rolls, 109
Pumpernickel Bread, 125–128
Pumpernickel Date-and-Walnut Bread, 129–130
Pumpkin and Olive Oil Loaf, Peppery, 140–142

quarry tiles, unglazed, 30–31

raisins
    Buttermilk Cinnamon-Raisin Bread, 143–145
    Chocolate-Raisin Babka Bundt, 226–228

Pumpernickel Date-and-Walnut Bread, 129–130
Turban-Shaped Challah with Raisins, 193–194
See also dried fruit
rancidity, 13, 22, 23
Raspberry Braid, 219–221
Raspberry Star Bread, 222–223
raw eggs, 20
raw sugar, 23–24
razor blades, 36
Red Pepper, Fougasse Stuffed with Roasted, 168–170
refrigerated doughs, 4–8, 43, 207
refrigerator rise technique, 53
resting times, 45–46, 50–52, 70–71, 240
rice/rice flours, 15–16
rising times, 50–51
Roasted Red Pepper, Fougasse Stuffed with, 168–170
roasting pans, 28–29, 59
rolling pins, 36
rolls, 108–115, 205–207
Rolls—With or Without Nuts, Sticky Caramel, 205–207
rosemary
    Focaccia with Onion and Rosemary, 163–164
Rosemary Crescents, 112–113
rum
    Chocolate-Raisin Babka Bundt, 226–228
rye flour, 14–15, 42, 75
    American-Style Whole Wheat Sandwich Bread, 134–136
    Deli-Style Rye Bread, 122–124

European Peasant Bread, 117–119
Pumpernickel Bread, 125–128
See also sourdough starters

salt, 20–21, 65, 75
Sandwich Bread, Gluten-Free, 175–176
scales, 37, 41–42
scoop-and-sweep method, 66
scoring/slashing, 71–72, 86
sea salt, 20
secret strategy, xiii
seeds, 23
  Bagels, 148
  Challah, 187–192
  Deli-Style Rye Bread, 122–124
  Not Rye, But So Very Close, 177–179
  Onion Pletzel, 165
serrated knives, 36, 37
sesame seeds, 23
  Bagels, 148
  Challah, 187–192
  750/1,000 rule, 76
shaping techniques
  Bagels, 146–148
  Brioche à Tête, 198–199
  Challah, 187–192
  Cinnamon Rolls, 208–210
  Fougasse Stuffed with Roasted Red Pepper, 168–170
  letter-fold bread-shaping technique, 90
  Olive Fougasse, 166–167
  Raspberry Braid, 219–221
  Rosemary Crescents, 112–113
  slashing, 71–72, 86

Soft Pretzels, 150–153
Sticky Caramel Rolls— With or Without Nuts, 205–207
tips and techniques, 7, 52, 85–115
Turban-Shaped Challah with Raisins, 193–194
Short-Cut Levain Loaves, 241
Sicilian-Style Pizza, 161
silicone mats, 34
"6-2-2-13" rule, 76
slashing/scoring, 71–72, 86
slicing tips, 35, 87
slow cookers, 105–107
small-quantity measures, 41–42
Soft Dinner Rolls, 108–109
Soft Pretzels, 150–153
Soft White Bread, Wondrous, 203–204
soggy crumb, 47–48
sorghum/sorghum flour, 16
  Gluten-Free Crusty Boule, 173–175
sourdough shortcut, 74, 241
sourdough starters, 57, 231– 237, 239
sponges, 6
spreading problems, 51
stainless steel containers, 32
stand mixers, 37–38
starters, 6
steam environment, 28–29, 30, 72–73
Stevia, 24–25
Sticky Caramel Rolls—With or Without Nuts, 205–207
Stollen, Christmas, 229–230
stones
  See baking stones/steels
storage containers, 32–33

storage life, 51, 53
storage recommendations, 4–8, 43, 55, 73–74
Strong White Dough, 77–78
Sufganiyot, 218
sugar, 23–24
Sunny-Side-Up Apricot Pastry, 211–213
sweeteners, 23–25, 82

table salt, 20
tapioca/tapioca flour, 16
  Gluten-Free Brioche, 180–182
  Gluten-Free Crusty Boule, 173–175
  Not Rye, But So Very Close, 177–179
tare, 37, 41, 42
teff/teff flour, 16
  Not Rye, But So Very Close, 177–179
temperature measures, 61
Thanksgiving Cornbread with Cranberries, Yeasted, 154–155
thermometers, 32, 73
thick-crust pizzas, 161
thin-crust pizzas, 161
tips and techniques, 41–61
  doughnut frying, 216–217
  gluten-free breads, 171– 172, 184
  loaf pans, 35, 87
  shaping techniques, 7, 52, 85–115
  sourdough starters, 236– 237
tomato toppings, 159
top crust problems, 48
Turban-Shaped Challah with Raisins, 193–194

unbleached all-purpose white flour, 12
unconventional seeds, 23
uncooked pizza sauce, 159
underbaking problems, 47–48
unfiltered water, 17
unglazed quarry tiles, 30–31

vanilla/vanilla beans, 211
vegetable oils, 21–22
vented containers, 33
Vermont Cheddar Bread, 137–139
vital wheat gluten, 13–14, 79, 80, 241
volume measures, 61

walnuts
    Pumpernickel Date-and-Walnut Bread, 129–130
    Sticky Caramel Rolls—With or Without Nuts, 205–207
warm bread, 50
water, 17, 19
water sprayers, 28
weights and measures
    American-Style Whole Wheat Sandwich Bread, 134–136
    Brioche, 195–197
    Buttermilk Cinnamon-Raisin Bread, 143–145
    Challah, 188
    Chocolate-Raisin Babka Bundt, 226–228
    Deli-Style Rye Bread, 122–123
    European Peasant Bread, 118
    Gluten-Free Brioche, 180–182

Gluten-Free Crusty Boule, 173–175
Light Whole Wheat Dough, 83
master recipe, 64
Not Rye, But So Very Close, 177–179
100% Levain-Risen Bread: White or Whole Wheat, 238–241
100% Whole Wheat Dough, 80
100% Whole Wheat Sandwich Bread with Milk and Honey, 131–133
Pain au Potiron (Peppery Pumpkin and Olive Oil Loaf), 140–142
Pumpernickel Bread, 125–126
Strong White Dough, 77
tips and techniques, 21, 41–42
Vermont Cheddar Bread, 137–139
Whole Wheat Brioche, 200–202
Wondrous Soft White Bread, 203–204
Yeasted Thanksgiving Cornbread with Cranberries, 154–155
wet doughs, 4–8, 12, 42, 43–44
Wheat Stalk Bread, 92–93
White Bread, Wondrous Soft, 203–204
white granulated sugar, 23
white rice flour, 16
white whole wheat flour, 13
whole wheat flour/breads

American-Style Whole Wheat Sandwich Bread, 134–136
Brioche, 200–202
Challah, 192
characteristics, 13–14
European Peasant Bread, 117–119
100% Levain-Risen Bread: White or Whole Wheat, 238–241
100% Whole Wheat Dough, 79–81
100% Whole Wheat Sandwich Bread with Milk and Honey, 131–133
Pain au Potiron (Peppery Pumpkin and Olive Oil Loaf), 140–142
storage recommendations, 13
variations, 81–82
Wondrous Soft White Bread, 203–204

xanthan gum, 16–17
    Gluten-Free Brioche, 180–182
    Gluten-Free Crusty Boule, 173–175
    Not Rye, But So Very Close, 177–179

yeast, 18–20, 65
Yeasted Thanksgiving Cornbread with Cranberries, 154–155
yeasty aroma, 57
yucca, 16

zero-out, 37, 41, 42
zesters, 38